PEACEFUL PARENTING AND MINDFULNESS FOR PARENTS AND KIDS

How to Use Mindful and Empowering Methods for a Joyful Family, Loving Home, and Outstanding Relationships

GRACE STOCKHOLM

TABLE OF CONTENTS

MINDFULNESS SIGNS: STAY IN THE MOMENT

(Before you continue to read, make sure to download your complimentary bonus)

Mindful enough? I hope you are!

With this download, you'll get 5 free printable signs that:

- Will immediately get you back to the present moment;
- Are specifically designed to bring awareness and mindfulness;
- Are easy to hang on a wall, stick on the fridge or anywhere else;
- Hang them everywhere, notice them, and come back to the now!

Mindfulness is a powerful tool for productivity, focus and calmness.

Go ahead and click on the link below to get your free mindful signs:

http://gracestockholm.net/peaceful-parenting-and-mindfulness-fridge-signs/

INTRODUCTION

Joyce Maynard once said, "It's not only children who grow. Parents do too. As much as we watch to see what our children do with their lives, they are watching us to see what we do with ours. I can't tell my children to reach for the sun. All I can do is reach for it myself."

You felt a deep love inside you the moment your child was born; however, parenthood is a challenge, especially in the first few years. It's a full-time job regardless of your age, gender, religion, culture, or profession. The bookstores are filled with parenting advice, some of which are great and others that don't work for us. Someone always has tips to provide us with the best parenting information on earth. Every parent has one aspiration in their lives, and that's to raise a child who can handle anything life has planned for them. They search endlessly for guidance on how to better their last effort or give their child a great start. There's only one problem we face. Each child is unique, and it can often take a compilation of multiple strategies to help our children reach the sun.

So often, the issue that arises from aimlessly using this compilation is that it doesn't work. Do you know why it doesn't work? The answer is the same reason for treating symptoms in an ailment without addressing the underlying cause. There is no rational reason why we will scratch the surface of any problems our children face and forget the ones buried deep inside. Some adults assume that children can't possibly feel anxious, insecure, fall prey to heartbreak, and allow the clutches of depression to consume them. The home becomes an arena where disputes are welcome and communication is nothing but mindless chatter. Their minds are uneasy, and these are the symptoms of this unrest. We can only alter their future by removing the root cause. In this case, we aim to begin and end with the mind.

The mind can't be tamed until we understand what's causing the interruption of silence in the first place. This noise is in our unconscious minds and incomprehensible to the untrained ear. It's been there since the day we were born, and we made peace with it. The problem is that we make peace with the enemy, and this can backfire. Mindfulness, alongside peaceful parenting, is the art of listening to this mixture of sound in our minds and translating it to a coherent tune. The two powerful techniques combine to yank us back to the present time. You can only listen to the present as you are fully aware of your environment and all that you're doing.

Parenting, washing the dishes, sitting in the office, driving to work, or even standing still can stop us from experiencing life. Life's many experiences are what make us human, and the only way we can enjoy it as individuals and families is to live it mindfully and peacefully. We can become the person we wish to be, and we can raise our children to be their best version. It's possible to transform your mind into a present, aware, and peaceful state with some simple practices. We all wish to grasp what life truly is about and acknowledge the things that matter most to us and the people around us.

A common issue among parents today is the anxiety of uncertainty and the unknown. There's a fear of what may happen, and in some cases, what has already happened. Children can be closed books at times, and parents suffer from terrible angst about what they might have done wrong. This disquiet in our minds can keep us distracted, and we fail to focus on doing our part as parents here and now. A fretful mind resonates throughout the family and doesn't only affect the parents. Children suffer from it as a secondary proxy.

Mindfulness has proven to reduce stress in the home and at work (Katz, n.d.). Living our lives mindlessly and parenting in the same fashion doesn't only pass our unsuitable behaviors onto our children; it also impacts their ideas and actions for the rest of their lives. Every time our children see us being crushed by anxious thoughts, they affiliate the contributors as a threat and will continue to do so. Turning a restless mind into a mindful intellect will help parents control themselves better, and this will provide the loving environment their children deserve.

The number of parents growing anxious about their kids is increasing dramatically. The reality is that we can't blame technology for this problem entirely. We live in a fast-paced world where dangers lurk around every corner. Our ability to cope with full schedules at home and work makes us vulnerable. It's easy to blow things out of proportion when we are overwhelmed like this.

Mindfulness has surpassed the notions of it being a trend. It isn't a mere subject of interest alone anymore. Peaceful parenting is the same. Mindful techniques and living are evidenced to relieve our stress, anxiety and depression and lessen the symptoms from physical ailments (Corliss, 2014). It's even used in cancer patients and people who suffer from heart conditions, among other physical problems. The same techniques will help you become a better version of yourself in every aspect of your life, not just parenting. Your career will be under less strain, your health will excel, and your bonds will grow stronger with your children and spouse.

By the time you reach the end of this book, I guarantee you'll:

- Have a new and complete understanding of what mindfulness and meditation is
- Have the power to switch to peaceful parenting and make intelligent calm decisions
- Be able to practice the ancient art of mindfulness with meditation and various other techniques to relieve stress and any other daily issues
- Find comfort in adversity by using different and valuable peaceful parenting techniques

3

- Have the ability to experience an enhanced and joyful life as a parent or family member
- Be equipped with one-minute, ten-minute, or longer duration meditations to use every day to implement the benefits thereof for the rest of your life
- Have the skills necessary to come back to the present in any situation or environment
- Have the attentive devotion required to focus on what needs to be done without the overwhelming stress anymore
- Become a better husband, wife, mother, father, or child in the comfort of a mindful home

Stores and online publishing platforms have been swamped with books of mindfulness and peaceful parenting over the last decade. I don't discount them, and I'm sure they offer good advice on the importance of mindfulness and practicing these methods for a better future. However, many of them don't address every aspect you need to create a wholesome family life through parenting, from babies through to the teenage years. With the help of this book, you'll have the tools you need to address every issue. I've used a concise methodology that's been tested time and again, offering extensive research available to prove my point.

I veer away from technical details and give you pragmatic and straightforward advice, using examples that frequent our lives as parents and children. Let me not forget about the exercises I share with you so that you can become the family member that everyone loves. There's nothing complicated about my guidance, and it can be followed by children who are at the beginning of their educational life as well. I've left no person behind and the practical information in this book can be used by mothers, fathers, teenagers, and young children.

Living mindlessly is the only complication in our lives. Our thoughts and feelings form the foundation of our discontentment and can lead to an utterly miserable existence. The mind is where everything begins, and we commonly fall prey to a seemingly simple, harmless thought.

Unfortunately, this snowballs into a massive mass that progresses into our mental and physical realm.

You know it's time to change the direction of this rolling snowball and release yourself from the avalanche of mindlessness. You yearn for the calmness that resides in a mindful person and wish to be present for every moment of life. You don't want to miss out anymore. Now is the time to begin your journey of learned success. If you wish to live a productive, happy, and peaceful life with your family, mindfulness, and peaceful parenting will get you there in no time!

CHAPTER 1:

MINDFULNESS: DEFINITIONS FROM THE MASTERS THEMSELVES

Mindfulness is still relatively foreign to the Western world, which we consider to be the leader of modern science and medicine. Hordes of people practice this technique of life and those who are unfamiliar with it often find themselves seeing it as leisure or spirituality. Yes, it can be both of these things, but it is also much more than this. It's not only Buddhists who sit in their temples and reach deep into a transient state, but it can also be the person who wishes to live a fulfilling life in their career, family, and emotional wellbeing. Let's take a look at how the masters define this practice.

Defining Mindfulness

There are varying definitions of mindfulness because it's complicated to put into words alone. It means various things and is experienced differently by various people. I will give you somewhat of a universal understanding of the word, but you will find additional meaning to it once you become familiar with it yourself.

Mindfulness is a practice, or as I like to call it, a way of life. It's the act of living mindfully and creating an attendance of mind. The mind that resides within your brain, as many experts believe, is a pliable being, to say the least. It is easily distracted and influenced by the fast-moving world around us. This ever-shifting presence of lifeforms and non-lifeforms that envelope us are responsible for directing our minds to something we call thoughts. The average human being doesn't experience a moment in their life when their mind isn't flooded with thoughts and distractions.

Many people suffer from a mindless presence, and mindfulness brings us back to the present. It allows us to attend what's happening around us fully, and we're able to see what we're doing, and even the very space we're moving through. It's part of the human condition to be born with a mind that is easily steered off the path we wish to be on. Often, we will need to focus on something of great importance, and our minds act like little children who haven't yet been disciplined. They have no direction, and we fail to call on them to pay attention to the task at hand.

We all can be fully aware of our environment at any given time and stop the cycle of falling into an overwhelming trap of overreaction to what's going on around us. We don't need to conjure the skill up from thin air because it's already present in our childlike minds. Just as we need to teach our children the basics of life and how to live it, we have to do the same with a foundational skill that already exists within our minds.

Think of your mindful state as being intrinsic at the moment. It lies dormant and needs to be brought to the surface with proven techniques and practices. It is as natural as an instinct once you've honed it to perfection and can be applied while you're sitting, standing, walking, and even driving. It is part of our animal instincts, and we only need to awaken it.

We can observe our minds from an introspective viewpoint when we practice the methods that wake this white elephant. We can use it to gain insight, awareness, reduce stress, enhance performance, and even become aware of other people's wellbeing. This is crucial to living a wholesome family life with relationships that remain consistent. This practice can remove the veil of judgment we have toward ourselves and our loved ones, and it provides us with the compassion we need to improve ourselves and be there for other people.

It doesn't matter if you're a chief executive officer (CEO) of some large corporation or a stay-at-home parent, you can achieve the accomplishments and life improvements that come from this spectacular application.

Interesting Facts

Many experts will agree on a few points when it comes to mindfulness. Anyone is capable of doing it, and it doesn't require a special kind of person. The way of life doesn't necessitate changes in your person or the people around you. There's nothing exotic or alien about the technique, and even science agrees that it can help us live in the moment. It's one method of bringing your innovation to the surface, and it helps us drive out any self-harming behaviors we've allowed in our lives until the point of mindful training.

Here are some beliefs about the practice that are commonly mentioned and which I would like to clarify.

Is Mindfulness Linked to Occults?

No, mindfulness has nothing to do with occult movements. You're most welcome to follow one of the many spiritual pathways that Buddhists, Hindus, and even Christians believe in, but there is no correlation to any occult divisions. Mindful states are historically connected to religion in some form or another, but they don't depend on spiritual worship. This is something you will choose if you please. You will not change your belief system if you believe in one God or another. Gautama Buddha is the famous Buddha that most replications and likenesses are connected to in Buddhism and remains the most famous Buddha of all time. His teachings have mentioned on numerous occasions that mindfulness is a way of life and not a form of worship. Spiritualism is a great booster for the technique, but the road you take is yours alone to choose.

Can My Whole Family Do This?

I've explained how this skill lies dormant in all our minds, and even children can activate the powers that lie within it. You don't need to learn a new skill because you're only disciplining one that already exists. You are aware of the ability that resides in your mind, but you've paid no attention to it before now. You will only change your routine and the outlook you have on life because you will see more than you were capable of doing before. You can help your children grow this talent in their minds from a young age; there's no need for theirs to lie dormant. Someone as young as five can practice this technique because their minds are already swamped with thoughts and behaviors that reflect on their thought patterns.

What If I Believe in Science Above Spiritualism?

Science has studied the effects of mindfulness, and the techniques linked to it to answer these questions. It has been used to confirm the improvement in individuals who suffer from anxiety and depression extensively. I will share some studies with you throughout the book to remove any doubts you might have about science and mindfulness. The beauty is that science is evidence-based, and that's why we enhance our faith in a strategy when something is supported with facts.

Mindful Leaders Explain the Phenomena

There are a few names that are synonymously famous in the realm of mindfulness. I would like to share their views with you so that you can acknowledge the opinions of people who've spent the majority of their lives in this lifestyle (Fondin, 2015). Many of these opinions are from gurus that are well-known today, and some of them are still practicing. The word guru comes from the Sanskrit language and translates to someone who "dispels darkness." Darkness needn't be the idea of evil in spiritualism. It can also relate to the darkness that clouds our judgment and keeps our thoughts running in one obscure direction.

The first guru is widely known as Amma, but her name is Mata Amritanandamayi. I'm sure you understand why we call her Amma. She was born in 1953 and still lives and teaches the mindful way of life today. The word Amma itself translates to "mother," and her followers see her as a mother-like figure. Many of her followers also refer to her as the hugging saint. Amma spends an astounding 22 hours a day helping people embrace this way of life when she's on tour. Her journey began when she was only nine and her mother became ill. She visited many homes in her village in pursuit of food and was struck with the reality of poverty when she saw these poor families. Her compassion took over, and she provided them with clothing and food from her home.

She would often embrace strangers with hugs and felt the pain that burdened these people with grief and sadness. Her embrace of men was often shunned upon in India as an adolescent, but she persevered. She has taught over a million followers the benefits of meditation today, and her organization has fed more than ten million poverty-stricken families in India. Her meditation is known world-wide as Integrated Amrita Meditation, or IAM. She learned the act of selflessness, or seva, and her definition of mindfulness strikes the heart. She believes that it's our number one duty to help our fellow beings in this world.

Sri Sri Ravi Shankar is the next guru on my list to share. He was born in India in 1956. He is known as the ambassador of peace and started an organization called The Art of Living Foundation. Sri Sri, as many call him, holds degrees in physics and Vedic literature and introduced the breathing technique called Sudarshan Kriya. His goal is to teach us how to live a stress-free life and embrace the art of living mindfully. He has even conveyed messages of peace to Iraq. The definition of mindfulness to Sri Sri is that we should be ready for any challenge. Readiness is what brings about happiness.

Eckhart Tolle is another guru that deserves admiration. He was born in Germany and studied in Cambridge. I'm sure you know who Paris

Hilton is; Tolle is the man that brought spirituality into her life. She admitted to reading *The Power of Now* while she was imprisoned. This man gets my recognition for this act alone even though he continues to teach mindful techniques around the world. Tolle defines mindfulness as living in the moment and is known as one of the greatest self-help gurus worldwide. He has taken inspiration from ancient Hindu texts and teaches Zen Buddhism. He explains that living in the present helps us overcome stress and doubts that plague our minds, and we can learn to enjoy the moment.

Wayne Dyer is another self-help guru that deserves credit. He continues to teach people about mindful living and improving their thought patterns. He has published over 30 successful titles to date. One that's received much attention is called *Change Your Thoughts, Change Your Life*. I've watched many of his videos, and he is truly an inspirational man. Dyer believes that we all have a little divinity inside of us and is famously linked to philosophies such as the *New Thought Movement*. He speaks of people who believe that their thoughts are gospel, and they shouldn't. We should challenge them and look at things in a new light. This includes any warped beliefs about ourselves. He defines mindfulness as changing the way we look at things and then those things will change.

The last guru I'll discuss is Deepak Chopra. His is a name most of us have heard. He was born in 1947 and still teaches today. He has been called the "poet-prophet of alternative medicine" by *Time Magazine* and has published over 80 self-help books on the mind-body connection. He uses modern forms of philosophy and teachings and is known to have helped millions of people around the world. Chopra began his journey as a medical doctor in Boston before he founded the Chopra Foundation. He was born in India and fantasized about becoming a famous writer. His father was a cardiologist and persuaded him to study medical science first. It was while he was chief of medicine at New England Memorial Hospital that he doubted Western medicine and its practices.

He started studying alternative medicine and followed the likes of Maharishi Mahesh Yogi, who taught transcendental meditation. His holistic approach expanded, and in 1996, he co-founded the Chopra Center for Wellbeing with doctor David Simon. He published a book called *Ageless Body, Timeless Mind*, that sold over a million copies, and he reached celebrity status. Doctor Simon got involved again and the two of them established a mantra-enforced meditation technique inspired by ancient Hindu texts. This meditation was called primordial sound meditation. He is well-known for guiding celebrities from Hollywood down the path of mindfulness and even taught Oprah Winfrey the valuable technique. Chopra has expressed his joy for meditation and describes waking up at four in the morning to spend two hours in a deep, mindful state. He teaches us to keep stillness inside of us amid chaos and movement.

There are many more inspirational gurus, but I'll stick with the handful I've mentioned to give you an understanding of the broad spectrum of definitions.

A Brief History: East to West

It's essential to know the history of a practice to understand how deep its roots dig into the lives of humanity. I'll give you a quick overview of its history. It begins in ancient Eastern philosophy and religion and extends its grasp into the Western world as we know it today.

Mindfulness is traced back thousands of years ago and even ages back before Jesus himself. It was practiced in many religious and traditional forms and could even be used on its own without a spiritual essence. The oldest recording of the practice dates back to Hinduism, and this makes the date of origin hard to establish. Hinduism has no singular founder, and it's considered the oldest religion in written history. It was never called Hinduism back then and consisted of various religious followings. The word Hinduism is a term we call it today and describes a massive religious movement in India based on Vedic traditions that were only coined as Hinduism in the 1800s.

The first record of religion, as we refer to it today, originates in the Indus Valley over 4,000 years ago. This region is known as Pakistan today. The teachings of these philosophers were written in the Vedic texts around 2,500 years ago when written scriptures became widespread. Additional texts were written that included the words dharma and worship in temples around this period. The Sanskrit translation for dharma has many meanings itself. One that I agree with is learning to live virtuously and in accordance with the order of the universe.

However, mindfulness isn't only found in Hinduism. Gautama Buddha was a teacher of this technique himself between 500 B.C. and 400 B.C. He was influenced greatly by the Hindus and even taught in their territory. Buddha strongly believed in the concept of dharma as well and taught us to live in harmony with the order of the universe or divine order of life. The two religions are somewhat falsely connected, as Buddhism doesn't follow the Veda scriptures, which are known as the holy texts of Hinduism.

Buddhism itself has branched into various religions, some of which are known as Theravada Buddhism, Zen Buddhism, and the famous Tibetan Buddhism we link to the Dalai Lama today. There's a broad understanding of sati in Buddhism, and this translates to mindfulness. It is taught among all the variations and is considered the initial step one must take to reach enlightenment. Western teachers often take inspiration from Buddhist monks, and this is why our modern version of the practice is credited mainly to Buddhism.

Many followers don't know how far and wide the technique reaches because it continued to be influenced by Judaism, Christianity, and Islam. The concept of dharma can relate to any of these religions, and they all require us to live by various definitions of what the universe and spiritual Gods consider the ordinance. Another practice that teaches mindfulness is yoga, and this has no direct ties to religion. Yoga itself has ties to Hinduism and what is known as the yoga sutra texts. We are familiar with yoga as a practice, and this dates back to 400 B.C. itself.

Now I want to clarify how mindfulness has traveled west. I'm going to take a giant leap forward and speak of Jon Kabat-Zinn, who was a professor of medicine in Massachusetts. He was born in New York in 1944 and continues to influence the world of alternative psychology. Kabat-Zinn studied mindfulness under numerous Buddhist monks, including the famous Thich Nhat Hanh. Hanh is another popular teacher of Western philosophy and alternative medicine in the world today.

Kabat-Zinn used his Eastern philosophical knowledge and combined it with Western medical science to create an eight-week program to reduce stress. This program is known as the Mindfulness-Based Stress Reduction (MBSR) program. He also founded the Center for Mindfulness at the University of Massachusetts Medical School and the Oasis Institute for Mindfulness-Based Professional Education and Training among other programs. Kabat-Zinn's integration of the East and West is when mindfulness genuinely gained momentum in Western society and was continually studied to confirm its validity.

Psychology took inspiration from this program and implemented a new one called Mindfulness-Based Cognitive Therapy (MBCT). This treatment option offered people a solution to the major depressive disorder that hinders many of us today. It was difficult for the Western world to recognize such a foreign idea like mindfulness, but science was used to aid the amalgamation of the two.

Furthermore, the Insight Meditation Society (IMS) was introduced by psychologists Jack Kornfield, Sharon Salzberg, and Joseph Goldstein in 1975. This program initiated the practice in clinical and non-clinical environments. Technology evolved to a point where we can measure and record the effectiveness of mindful practices in psychology and leisure fronts. It is commonly used to reduce stress so that we can live wholesome lives with ourselves and others. This is how mindfulness has birthed the techniques we commonly use today to overcome obstacles that come onto our paths. No one is immune to these obstacles, and the moment modern technology and practice agreed with ancient Eastern philosophy, a new era was born.

CHAPTER 2:

PEACEFUL PARENTING: A BETTER WAY OF RAISING KIDS

This might appear as another foreign concept to parents or individuals. You might also be familiar with the concept already and need some additional guidance. Peaceful parenting is a fairly new strategy that helps you raise children who will undoubtedly thrive in the modern world. It is a new type of parenting that brings the parents and the children to "one table" because a family cannot live fulfilling lives if everyone is in disunity. Let's have a look at the introductory details of this revolutionary parenting style that bonds families in a way they never thought possible. I'll dive deeper into the information further in the book.

Peaceful Parenting

You will be questioning what this style of parenting is if you're new to the notion, but I'll elaborate on the particulars for you. Think about the common problem we face as parents and families today. There's a constant war between us and our children that can leave us feeling like an army general at times, whether subtle or significant. We find ourselves falling into the familiar dictatorship that our forefathers have taught us because it's all we know. The problem is that children evolve, just as the world does, and the same approach isn't working anymore.

It's more harmful than we think and sends our children into a world unprepared for what goes on there.

Spanking our children or shouting at the top of our lungs only helps us lose respect from our kids. Think about your boss for a moment and acknowledge the amount of respect you feel for them after they barked at you for an honest mistake. It's also not uncommon for us to hear the words, "just because you were a so and so doesn't mean I should be." Our children like to be acknowledged as unique individuals, and they are offended by our comparison of the problems they face today to the issues we faced way back when. This is unfortunately true, and their problems are not the same that we had to deal with, so why should our parenting imitate the style of our ancestors?

The world is forever evolving, and so are our children. Every generation is different, and we need to adapt to the changes taking place around us. The bottom line is that we are simply waging a war on our own families by being ignorant of the evolution of society. The word peace has an intricate meaning on its own. It's time to raise your white flag and sign the treaty now by adopting a new approach to your kids, and even to your spouse.

Mindfulness plays a significant role in peaceful parenting because this type of parenting also teaches you to stop and look at what's going on right now. You cannot grasp fragments of information from your past, which was decades ago, and expect the same order of events to take place. The war will never come to an end if you do this. Family feuds can take its toll on the happiness of every family member, and the only way to overcome this is by becoming a peaceful person yourself. Change always begins with you, and you can't expect to see modifications in other people until you embrace the waves of transformation yourself.

Peaceful parenting introduces parents, new and old, to a concept of shifting time to here and now before they approach the situation calmly and use a set of tools to reach a solution. There is a specific dynamic you need to institute between a child and parent to create an unbreakable bond. One where they see you resonating a different approach to life and improving your behavior before you expect theirs to change. Children tend to follow the example of their parents, and they are frequently mimicking our behavior. I'm going to teach you the ground rules of this technique so that you can remove any hostilities from your home.

The Trinity of Peaceful Parenting

I call it the trinity of peaceful parenting because this style relies on three cornerstones, or constant reminders, that we need to institute in our homes and lives daily. It doesn't matter what the situation is; you can apply these rules to your parenting from this point on.

Parental Emotional Regulation

The first foundation is set upon our emotional regulation as parents. We need an introspection into the emotions that drive us and the reactions that come from them. Think about the time your son's school called because he got in a fight. What was the first emotion you reacted upon, and how did you respond when you saw him in the principal's office? For many, it's raging mad and barely controlling the outburst that followed the meeting. You might have grounded your son for five weeks straight because he gave another kid a bloody nose. This situation isn't helpful because your son might have punched the other kid out of rage, and now, you're showing him that his emotional response is correct by modeling the same.

Take a moment and pause before you blow your top and say something to your son that you can't take back. Words can be like a knife to the heart and are often remembered for ages to come. Come to silence, and deconstruct the issue before you react. Ask yourself why your son was enraged. Was he provoked before he hit the child? You should consider if there were any instigators and whether he was protecting something he believed in. Anger is often thought of as a secondary emotion to fear. Maybe he was defending himself. Think about the meeting in the principal's office and all that was said before you react to your son.

You want to set an example for your son, no matter why he became angry. The moment you erupt, you're sending him a message that his actions are tolerable. This doesn't mean that you can't share your anger, but you need to compose yourself mindfully before you do. This will help you decide whether you explode and shout at the top of your voice or if you sit down and discuss the issue with your son. Yes, he should know that you're upset by his behavior, but there's no need for the entire neighborhood to know your family's business. I've been guilty of losing my stuff before, and it sets a poor example for my children. Not to mention the embarrassment that we cause our children, and this breaks down their self-esteem.

Your moment of introspection gives you the time to sort through all possible reactions and choose one that is appropriate. I've watched parents scream at their children, and they don't realize that their children are screaming back because we become our parents. This part of the trinity can also be called the center because you are working on yourself before you radiate your influence onto your kids. Think about the person you want your child to be and model this person for them.

A Healthy Bondage

The second principle of peaceful parenting is the connection you have with your child. Many parents think they are connected with their children, but I'm speaking of a deep level of unity. The kind where we are intimately bonded to them.

There's a difference between helicopter parenting and closeness as well. Don't get the two confused. The best way to encourage your child to follow in your footsteps is to have the kind of relationship other people wish they had. This is when a parent and their kid are on the same wavelengths and present themselves in similar fashions. The children carry the morals and high ground that their parents do. Your children should see you as a role model, and this is how they'll pick up on your mindful way of life.

You will see that families who have this closeness between them have fewer rivalries in the home, and they tend to get along. This doesn't mean they never disagree, but they can reach an understanding easier than a parent and child who have no connection to each other emotionally and physically. The only way we can connect this way with our children is to spend time with them. Get to know them and learn about all the things that make them tick. Their interests and their fears are what motivates their thoughts and drive passion inside them. Be a part of that passion, play a game with them once in a while, or watch a movie they enjoy.

It's not just about spending time with them, either, because it's up to you to choose the right environment for them. Allowing your children to bear witness to chaotic environments will make them believe that chaos is welcome. You are installing distorted belief systems in your children from the time they are born if you allow them to be in an environment that teaches them that chaos is their reality. Work on providing them with the correct external influences and be an active parent to create the bond you desire.

Don't allow them to spend time in situations that belittle them or make them doubt their skills. Encourage their talents and remove them from any situation where their talents are questioned. Don't allow a music teacher to tell your daughter that she blows the clarinet like a foghorn when she is only learning to play the instrument. Look for positive influences in their life and support their decisions on what they choose to do.

You can also include daily rituals from a young age to bond the entire family. Introduce dinner as a shared experience from the time they can remember. Get involved in your child's sports at school and create fun family nights at least once a week when you can all choose an activity. Showing your child that you value their interests is one powerful method of connecting with them on that deeper level.

Communication Relations

I think it's safe to say that communication is key to any relationship we will ever enter. This relates to our marital relationship, our children, friends, family, and even our colleagues. It's no surprise that communication is the third foundational setting for peaceful relationships in the home. It all comes back to setting an example for your child again. You want clear and concise communication between you and your partner, including any other people your children know.

The same applies to communicating with your children. You want to coach them, rather than control them, from the onset of their lives. Be open with them and listen to the words they speak because you never want to cut the interaction you have with them. I'll return to the son who punched a classmate at school. The only way you'll get to the truth of the story is if you have an open line of communication from the get-go.

Let your child know that they can speak to you, and never shoo them away or treat their words as insignificant. We all want to be heard and that's a common denominator in human beings. Listen to his side of the story and let him explain why he became so angry in the first place. You might be surprised to know that he was protecting a young boy who had been bullied endlessly in his class. He finally stepped up because his reality is different from the bullies that walk around the school, stuffing smaller children in their lockers.

He explains how the teachers have done nothing about this bully since he has been in the school himself. This can enlighten an opportunity for you to return to the school and set an example when you discuss this with the principal. You might ask to involve the parents of the bully, as well as the parents of the young boy who is constantly beaten up at school. Don't just listen to your child. You should act on what they say, but use the first principal of this parenting style to think thoroughly about the best outcome for a good line of communication between all parties involved. Strong communication between you and your child will ensure that they build the all-too-valuable problem-solving skills we need in life because you can find a solution together.

The three foundational rules will apply to any situation and should remain consistent throughout the upbringing of your children. You shouldn't allow moods to sway and connections to be lost. This includes the relationship you have with your spouse. Any situation that presents itself can be modified to apply the rules mentioned here.

The Positivity Movement

Peaceful parenting is merely a philosophical resemblance of dharma, if you think about it. It requires parents to live life consciously in the present and to abide by the laws of nature. It helps us differentiate the good from the bad and gives us the tools to follow the way of life we want our kids to follow.

Parenting without punishment is related to the three foundations we discussed. We find our calm in that moment of silence in which we ponder all options and contributors to the circumstance in front of us. This movement teaches us to control our anger and manage it in a serene space in our minds. Punishing kids for whatever they do will become a non-existent negative ritual in this space, and this is how the positivity movement begins.

The fact is that you can't create a positive team effort in the family if there are temporary punishments, rewards, and threats. How does one create the relationship we spoke of when there is no trust? The three steps will help you create trust between yourself and your children. Fear-based obedience has short-term effects on a child, and the only way for them to want to change is when they become co-operative, self-disciplined, emotionally intelligent, and grow integrity. You want to foster mutual respect rather than raise children who dread you.

Removing punishment from their lives allows them to make decisions based on their self-discipline and integrity rather than their fear of punishment or their distorted belief that reward is necessary for their behavior. The world doesn't work this way, and as adults, they'll fail because their expectations of others are too high. We know that there's no reward for good behavior in adulthood, and having this expectation in inappropriate circumstances can lead to disappointment.

Your child should understand wrong from right because you have been concise in your instructions with them. You are allowed to set limits, but you need to make sure that the limits are understood. Do not mistake peaceful parenting as permissive parenting. It is simply a mutual understanding in which the child and parent benefit from the style simultaneously.

Remember that children who act out are crying for support or attention. This wouldn't be an issue if there remains a line of interaction between you, and you spend time listening to what they have to say. A child will not cry for no reason, and you should talk to them. They could be hungry, or an older child might be concerned about an exam they have the next day. Punishing them will break the bond that you've created. The son who hit his classmate would resent his parents for punishing him because he grew up with certain morals, and those ethics told him that it was wrong for the bully to bash the small boy around. Do you really want him to second guess his idealistic core beliefs? Those came from you, after all, when he saw you stand up for the underdog before. It's an admirable moral to stand up for the little guy.

Parents who follow the rules of peaceful parenting will avoid the war zone and gain the mutual respect they desire. There will be no need for chastisement and forceful correction if the relationship stands where it should. Teach your child the satisfaction of this positive outlook on life and that there's no challenge that can't be sorted out by the household. The balance shifts from power struggles to a family who sits down and solves issues together.

The Origins of a Valuable Technique

Laura Markham once said, "The most important parenting skill is managing yourself." Doctor Laura Markham from Columbia University qualified as a clinical psychologist who doubles as a mom. She has published three hugely successful parenting titles since she began the movement toward peaceful parenting herself. The books are *Peaceful Parent: Happy Kids: How to Stop Yelling and Start Connecting, How to Stop the Fighting and Raise Friends for Life,* and *The Peaceful Parent: Happy Kids Workbook.*

She has taken a shining to parenting styles and coaches parents from around the world. Her news articles reach more than 140,000 readers a week. She also spends time on the expert panel of Mothering.com and Pregnancy.com. She carries out interviews on various radio stations and has made the *Fox Morning Show,* among countless others. Doctor Markham confesses that it was parenthood that made her realize how hard it is to be a mom or dad. She describes parenting as the hardest job there is because there is often a lack of the tools or information required to excel at it.

Doctor Markham's aspiration is to support parents, one family at a time. She is the founder of *Aha! Parenting.* This website is filled with information and advice on moments we often say aha to. She lives in Brooklyn, New York, with her two sons who were raised happily with peaceful parenting and continues to teach others how to raise successful, happy children.

She has referred to her parenting style as a relationship-based tactic and has helped thousands of families across the United States and Canada. Her guidance has focused on issues relating to separation anxiety, cheekiness, mobile phone obsession, and sleeplessness. She is an inspiration to parents, and her techniques embrace the reality of mindfulness because we need to alter our minds to change our futures.

CHAPTER 3:

MINDFULNESS FROM A TO Z

Mindfulness is larger than previously discussed. I've explained how mindfulness can't be described in simple words. The definition of it is vast and complicated. I'll go into further detail in this chapter by pointing out introductions to the main aspects of the "mindfulness alphabet" because it doesn't only involve meditation.

Awareness

The A in our mindfulness alphabet represents awareness of yourself, your surroundings, and increasing alertness. Have you noticed how alcoholics must become aware of their problems before they can do something about them? I know it's a harsh example, but it states the facts. We need to become alert to our surroundings and what's going on in and around us at all times. Mindfulness teaches us to do just that when we focus intently on our emotions and the responses that come from them.

One method of reaching a new level of this stage is to keep a journal. Whenever something happens that ticks you off, you can jot it down in your journal. You will broaden your awareness relating to an emotional response and can even look at various strategies to correct it. Writing is therapeutic on its own, and when our words touch down on the paper, we can see things clearly. It's similar to taking a moment to breathe before you respond emotionally to something. Our written words bring us to the present time and help us observe the memories while they're fresh in our minds. There's nothing like a silent room with a pen and paper to bring you to a heightened level of self-awareness.

Daydreams

Daydreaming seems to come naturally to children, but we forget how to do it when we grow older. Or so we think. Daydreaming and fantasizing are the same thing and when we sit there with our minds in another realm, we imagine ourselves doing something or reaching for something. It allows us to conjure up an image in our minds that we use to elaborate on a task at hand or something we would like to achieve. Adults don't stop daydreaming. We just call it something else. Our thoughts wander off into another space and time.

This isn't the worst thing because it can give us time to ponder on how to complete a task or find a solution to a problem we couldn't see before. Creativity is enhanced in children because a different, previously dormant part of their brain becomes active when they pretend to play or live in their imaginative worlds (Taylor et al., 2015). Never tell your child to stop daydreaming again. The only important note to mention here is the fact that we should imagine quality. It doesn't help to fantasize about unrealistic goals because this isn't improving your mindfulness. See the goal at hand and daydream about it with every part of your body. Get involved in your dream state and allow your imagination to pinpoint the solutions and steps needed to reach the target you see.

Feeling

I'm sure this word is explanatory on its own. The feeling aspect of mindfulness lies within acknowledging your emotions and not avoiding them. You want to feel the emotion because it can be a conduit to something residing in your subconscious mind. I know that some emotions are just painful, but we can't overcome something when we hide away from it. These feelings are often a precursor or an after effect of something that needs attention. You need to stop suppressing your anxiety and embrace it, however painful it may be in the beginning. There's nothing wrong with having emotions. It's part of being human.

People who become mindful will learn to regulate their emotions rather than shoving them aside. Emotions are a response from thoughts, and sometimes, they can be related to memories. Feelings walk hand-in-hand with the experiences that you've encountered. They can even belong to someone else. Have you ever had your child tell you that their teacher neglects them and that they don't know how they'll pass this semester if they can't find an answer? Your child is hurting, and the emotion passes on to you when you feel the agony of parental care across your heart. Emotions can reveal answers to problems as well, and this situation must be dealt with. Obviously, you'll spend time thinking about all the possible solutions before you head over to the school, but it's fine to allow yourself to feel the pain and anger from this. The only way you can learn to regulate feelings is by embracing them when they come along.

Gratitude

Gratitude is one thing that evades us often. Human beings are so set on finding the greener grass that belongs to their neighbor that we often overlook the immaculate lawn on our side of the fence. Take a closer look over the fence, and you might notice that it looks greener because it's full of clovers. Clovers are weeds and don't belong in the grass. Anyway, we are always aiming to reach for the stars and fail to see the silver lining that resides within us already. Gratitude is one technique that will be difficult and requires much practice, but it remains a key aspect of being mindful.

Forget about your sister, who was promoted to a new branch in the city and now gets a company vehicle and a paid-for apartment. Look at yourself and think about all the little things. Find happiness in what you have. It doesn't mean that you should stop striving for greatness, but you should end the cycle of setting yourself up for emotional failure. You have beautiful children and a spouse that loves you. You might not drive a Bentley from Germany, but your car gets you and your family to where you need to be. Be thankful for what you have and never stop looking for reasons to be grateful for the achievements you've accomplished thus far. You are not at the end of your story yet, and it can continue in a smoother direction.

Practicing gratitude can enhance your physical, mental, and emotional health. Teach your kids to be content with their lives and stop being hard on themselves for what they think is underachievement. You will thrive in the workplace and your family life, and your self-esteem will burst through the ceiling when you learn to be content in life.

Listening

This mindful aspect makes me think of how women are generalized on television. There is always a lady who is fighting with her husband or partner about not listening to them. The partner will simply nod their head in agreement even when the woman speaks of how she's about to key her husband's car. This is a poor generalization because difficulty to really listen and hear someone else is common among women and men who haven't become mindful yet. The entertainment provided by these sitcoms is often hilarious, but they can touch a subject that's only partially true. The only difference is that we all suffer from this.

Listening is difficult because our lives are constantly distracted by noises, emotions, and interruptions. When was the last time you listened to yourself? Your body speaks to you, and so do your thoughts, emotions, and desires. Learn to listen to yourself and then listen clearly to the people around you. Practice your skills until you can hear every word your partner shares with you, and vice versa. It plays a role in communication and is the groundwork for healthy and long-lasting relationships. You want wholesome relationships to become a close-knit family and reach a peaceful and mindful state. Besides, you will uncover secrets in your mind and the minds of your family when you listen to them intently.

Meditation

Meditation is one of the most widespread techniques of reaching and sustaining mindfulness. It is the method of training your mind into the desired format. Meditation gives you access to your inner mind, or subconscious, where ideas are born and raised like children. Your subconscious mind is the conscious level that is most susceptible to suggestions, and becoming a mindful person or family is, in fact, a suggestion that needs to be reared by your unconscious mind. It is the part of your brain that functions at speeds that our conscious minds are unable to. It's where thoughts, emotions, and responses originate.

The practice isn't a singular art form and requires a compilation of concentration, focus, guidance, and imagination. People find it challenging to sit for long periods of time and empty their minds from all distractions that linger in the environment, and that's why I call it a form of art. Guided imagery meditation is the best place for someone to implement this exercise in their daily routine, as it helps you reach the level of relaxation that is needed for awakening the subconscious mind.

There are various kinds of meditation that you can try. The first is called concentration meditation, and this is when you focus on one thing until it becomes the only thing on your mind. Voice-guided meditations help you do this because you focus intently on the voice you hear. It can also involve concentrating on your breathing until your body falls into the ultimate level of comfort. Some people use mantras or the sound of a gong to shift their attention from all the interruptions that love hindering us during our peaceful silence.

The second kind of meditation I'd like to mention is mindfulness meditation itself. This form is famous for breaching your awareness and observation. You are also guided into a calm state where the subconscious takes over, and you observe the thoughts that move through your mind like a speeding train. This method can be mastered as your observation increases, allowing you to slow down these thoughts to acknowledge them and see them for what they truly are. There's no involvement or interruption from yourself, and you merely watch them pass by. This technique helps you find a balance when you recognize patterns that shouldn't be present in your mind.

Other kinds of meditation open yourself to compassion, for yourself and the people around you. All you have to do is reanalyze the processes in your mind and treat the responses kindly. Some meditations include tai chi, yoga, and walking meditation. The benefit of mastering this technique is that you'll be able to apply it in any situation, even when you're stuck in traffic. You can always use meditation to open your mind and look into the details of the present time. This ancient practice doesn't only help you take control of your mind; it also improves physical symptoms that might be present. You can lower your heart rate and blood pressure, lessen anxiety and stress, and find the relaxation you deserve. I'll go into fact-based details later in the book.

Peace

I've introduced you to the guru Eckhart Tolle before. He explains that peace is one of the major players in mindfulness (Newman, 2012). It's not possible to have peace if we don't appreciate the things we have in our lives. Our judgment can become clouded when we fail to see the good in situations or people, and this happens because we can't see the good in ourselves. Peace is a state of ultimate liveliness and should never be confused with unconsciousness. People think they can drink to overcome their emotions but then realize that the emotions didn't go anywhere the next day. We can't sleep our thoughts away either because they'll simply return when we wake up.

There's also the delusion that peace equals happiness. This isn't entirely true because happiness can be defined as a temporary state where you get "high" on the circumstances around you. Change comes and our gleeful attitudes fade away. Peace is a deeper level of contentment, one that lasts for a long time. Peace comes from acceptance and understanding of the everyday disasters that befall us when we learn to cope with them and avoid them overwhelming us. Our peace can often be disrupted by past experiences and future concerns. We find it once we learn to steer clear of anything that doesn't belong in the present. Trusting yourself and your ability to remain mindful will help you stay on the path.

Rest

Rest is the next contributor to mindfulness. We live in a world that is constantly moving forward and waits for no one. However, rest for the mind and body is essential to keep our minds and bodies at peak health. Life is challenging, to say the least, and we commonly enter the rut of burning the candle at both ends. We feel as though we need to finish everything today, and we forget that tomorrow is another day. Yes, I teach you about the present moment, but what is your body telling you at that moment when you feel like you've been running full steam ahead for the past two days?

Our minds and bodies are fragile, and we should listen to them when they tell us it's time for a break. This applies to both mental and physical exhaustion. A mindful person will prevent fatigue from reaching this stage by using practical resting periods to enhance their performance. It doesn't feel great when you force your mind to work overtime. You can often imagine the smoke coming from your ears, and your focus is below par when you reach this level of exhaustion. Take the time to rest when you need to and spend 10 to 20 minutes a day in a silent retreat of your choosing. This can include meditation, complete silence, locking your phone away, scheduling time for activities, reading a book, and even pursuing a hobby that relaxes you. There are no limits on how much rest you need, but your body will tell you. Keep track of how much time you feel you need to get a sense of your necessary rhythm.

Time

Time is an essence of this universe that we cannot easily manipulate unless we're in the present moment. We have, unfortunately, not invented time travel yet, and the moment you realize that now is all you have is the moment your mind finds peace. The past is an attraction for our mind to visit, and the future is the reason for our anxiety, fear, and any distress. The problem is that we can't change them. Even if you want to alter your future, the way you do it is by implementing a change now.

Time travel doesn't exist, and neither do fortune-tellers, in my opinion. No one can predict tomorrow, and life could throw you with lemon after lemon. That lemon won't strike you in the future because the moment it hits you is the present. The world is filled with distractions that are trying hard to remove our mindful state, and life is one of those.

Death is a terrible reminder of how we can't regain the time we've lost. We know that we can never hug the person again or even speak to them on the phone. Their presence in this world had come to an end when their time ran out. I know this is a grim example, but it's the most eye-opening of them all. The grim reaper comes at any moment, and what happens at this moment is what defines us. There's no peace in guilt, anger, grief, or even sadness when someone leaves this world. Grief itself is the consequence of losing time because the person we lost existed in a time we can never regain.

I love the saying that every moment in our lives counts for something. This is true, and to move away from the grave topic of death, we must live in the moment. We can change our future by starting to define our meaning in the present time. Yes, mindfulness takes practice, as anything in life does. However, we can begin our journey now so that the future doesn't look so scary anymore. All the introductions in this chapter will set you on the path to living in the present and using time to your advantage.

Zen

I'm sure you've heard the word Zen before. It relates very much to dharma. It's the act of living in harmony with nature, people, and all living things. It's the deepest level of peace and tranquility one can reach in our soul. There are no religious ties necessary, and the only way to practice Zen is to do just that. You should be practicing your discipline to the guidance in this chapter and be patient while you reach mindfulness. Nothing that we want in life has ever been gained without perseverance.

Think about the incredible value mindfulness can add to your family and how healthy your children can grow up, mentally and physically. Set your eyes on the target you wish to achieve, and this will ignite the motivation you need for practice. You need to cultivate the dedication one needs for repeated practice and never give up.

Zen focuses on breathing and sitting silently in the moment as our awareness expands to bring our minds closer to enlightenment. Zen practices or meditation can help you fixate on breathing and the movements of your body while you count to ten or back to one. This increases your ability to focus when there's something that needs deeper thought. You will learn to place your hands and sights in the right position to reach the ultimate position for meditation. A seated Zen practice requires grounding your body in the present space and keeping your spine erect. There are also walking Zen techniques, and you can use mantras to enhance your meditation. It's another form of observing ourselves and the way we think, act, and feel. We will learn more about the details soon enough.

CHAPTER 4:

MEDITATION:
THE KEY TO A MINDFUL LIFE

I've spoken about meditation on and off throughout the book, but now it's time to give you another definition of it. I'll also introduce you to the facts that coincide with the technique and to what extent this practice can benefit you and your family. There are various methods and durations for the meditation that suits you best, and some can help someone who is new to the practice.

Mindful Submission Explained Further

How do various religions and cultures define meditation? The word itself means the act of thinking deeply. The word meditation came about when the technique moved from the East to the West. That means that the word is a modernized description. If you look up the definition of philosophy, you will find another interesting fact that confirms the meaning because philosophers were deeply involved in meditation. One synonym for a philosopher is a thinker. Someone who spends time teaching philosophy to others is actually teaching them their thoughts and what previous thinkers have taught before them. Thinking is how we come to conclusions and make decisions. Meditation explains how thinkers used thought to clarify their minds and reach a higher understanding.

Buddhists practice meditation for the purpose of reaching Nirvana. Nirvana is the enlightenment our minds reach when we understand the truths of the universe and connect to the spiritual realm. They use it alongside two other methods to reach their ultimate spiritual connection. Christians, on the other hand, see this technique as a contemplative mode of prayer to create a union with God. Some might say it's a silent form of prayer or communication with God.

I've explained how meditation helps you reach your subconscious mind, and this is where the thoughts are running amok. These thoughts are created by memories, and the fragments of likeness that stir thoughts are the culprit behind unwanted contemplations. Use the practice of thinking deeply and slowing your thoughts down to expose yourself to them and reap from the benefits that come from it.

Meditation is a practice on its own and shouldn't be confused with other techniques. It can use other exercises to promote your connection to mindfulness, but it remains a ritual on its own.

Various Types of Meditation

There are seven major types of meditation that you can practice to attain mindfulness. Some of them are used for beginners, and others are used when we reach an advanced stage of mindfulness. There are also techniques one can use for more powerful benefits. I've briefly discussed some of them, but I'll elaborate further now. Keep in mind that each of these has its own subtypes and that there are dozens of kinds in the world.

The first type is called Metta meditation and is commonly referred to as loving-kindness meditation. This is a form of compassionate practice that teaches you to show kindness to yourself, your loved ones, other people, a source of stress, and even an enemy. People use this type to focus on their breathing while they open their minds to compassion before sending it into the area it needs to be. It helps people overcome anger, interpersonal conflict, stress, depression, and frustration, to name a few challenges.

Progressive relaxation meditation is the next on my list of interests. This type is commonly used to relieve ourselves of tension by scanning our bodies progressively. You will focus on tension in a certain area of your body and pay attention to the release thereof. It's best to start at one point, such as your feet, and move your way up to your neck and head. You can tense your muscles before relaxing them again and visualize your tension as a physical form. This type is excellent in sleep-inducing exercises and relieving chronic pain.

Mindful meditation has been discussed, but I'll review it briefly again. The main focus is to remain aware and focus on the present. You become alert to your present surroundings and aim at removing judgment from your mind. Walking meditation can be combined with mindful meditation, and you can even carry this out in the grocery store. Take note of the checkout line and the people around you to ground yourself back in the present. It improves focus, memory, and relationship satisfaction. It reduces negative thoughts, responses, and impulsive actions.

Breath awareness meditation is the fourth main kind of practice. This is a subtype of mindfulness meditation as well, and all you need to do is focus on your breathing. Your attention must shift from stray thoughts and remain with the sound or feeling of your air intake. You can even count your breaths to keep within the guidelines of this technique. It reduces anxiety and improves emotional flexibility and concentration. It also acts as the baseline for most meditation practices.

Kundalini yoga is another art form of ancient practices. This is a form of meditation in which specific movements are combined with mantras or chanting to reach a mindful state. The movements can be learned at home, or you can join a class. This form of meditation relieves stress and anxiety to improve your mental acuity. It also reduces pain and increases your physical strength as a bonus.

Zen meditation earns its own right as well, but is best practiced at an advanced level or under the guidance of a practitioner. A teacher can help you achieve the correct posture and follow the specific steps that involve opening the chakras. This is merely a more disciplined form of mindfulness meditation and isn't the best option for beginners. It bridges the gap between spiritualism and relaxation.

Transcendental meditation is the final major partaker. This form is used for powerful intervention and connects you spiritually. A teacher will guide you to transcend above your current state of being with advanced breathing and relaxation techniques. The chanting of mantras is required, but a teacher must determine which to use. They will use your year of birth and their year of training as an example, but this will be combined with various other complex factors. Modernized versions allow people to use a reflective type where they repeat words like, "I am the person I ought to be." This is an affirmation and not actually a mantra. You are also not transcending if you haven't reached a profound stage of mindfulness and spirituality. I suggest working toward this greater mindfulness by adding spirituality into the mix and finding a teacher who can take you on in person.

Meditation and Health

I've promised some rock-hard evidence to prove the benefits of meditation and mindfulness to your health. Let's begin with a problem that affects many of us. Depression and anxiety are common in our modern society, and they are often targeted by meditation or mindfulness-based stress reduction programs. Cancer is another topic we don't like discussing, but there have been significant improvements in cancer patients and survivors who have suffered from mental distress after treatment. I've found evidence that knocks them out of the park altogether.

I came across a meta-analysis that collected the data from 124 clinical trials conducted between 2000 and 2018 (Mehta et al., 2019). One of the studies included 166 women diagnosed with breast cancer who suffered from mood disorders, depression, and anxiety. It was a five-year longitudinal study in which the women were divided into two groups. The first was a group who were provided with meditation and MBSR programs at home and in weekly group sessions. The control group wasn't given meditation exercises and was treated with alternative programs. The results showed a significant decrease in mood disorders in the MBSR group. This article provides us with various examples from the 124 trials conducted.

Mood disorders or emotional distress in people can lead to serious complications if not halted. We all succumb to that moment that engraves depressive moods in our brain, and when left untreated, we can cause complications in our relationships, and our lives fall apart. This isn't the way we live mindfully as a family.

Physical symptoms and consequences can hinder our lives and happiness further. Or should I say it can hinder our peace? We lose sleep, gain high blood pressure, increased heart rates, and can suffer from horrendous anxiety attacks. We don't want to allow these issues to overwhelm our lives, and living mindfully will keep these things out of our families.

Learning How to Meditate

There is guided advice to achieve the best benefits from meditation. This involves the steps you take before you go into that mindful state. Posture, breathing, and focused thinking is the key to meditation. It is best to sit when you begin meditation because you don't want your mind to wander off or fall asleep when you're lying down. Sitting also helps to remove the mental processes in your brain when it must decide where to place your feet.

I began my journey with crossed legs because you don't want a reason to fail. Skilled practitioners sit on their haunches sometimes, and this places strain on your knees. Use the easy pose from yoga to start meditating. This involves resting one foot on top of the other leg. Your back should be straight because your spinal column is the link to the ground and the universe or spiritual space above you. Keeping this aligned correctly allows for a better flow through your entire body.

Focus on your breathing when you begin. Take deep but long breaths through your nostrils and always hold the air for a second as it fills your lungs. Purse your lips to expel the air gently through your mouth and use an elongated push to empty your lungs. Pay attention to the rise of your chest and stomach as you inhale and the fall of them when you exhale.

Your intention is to quiet the mind, but this doesn't mean thoughts won't pop in. Thoughts will grow louder and invade your mind space rapidly during meditation. Your body should remain relaxed and awake through the process. Your thoughts will run to every concern you have or any task needed to be completed. The way you silence the mind is by focusing closely on your breathing. Your mind continues to stay alert while counting breaths or even listening to them. This redirects the mind away from processing new thoughts.

My final advice is to dress comfortably and remove noisy distractions from your meditation space. Remember the advice on how to meditate when we enter the following meditations.

One-Minute Session

Meditation doesn't have to be a drawn-out process, and you can begin with short one-minute sessions. Focus on the process of meditating and not on the amount of time spent in a session. Find yourself seated as I described in the previous section and begin.

Close your eyes and take a deep breath in through the mouth and feel your lungs expand as the fresh air tickles its walls. Keep focusing on the cooling sensation in your breath as thoughts move swiftly in front of you. Press the air out of your mouth gently and feel as the stress exits your body. The stress that ties itself to those fast-moving thoughts leaves in the flow of your breath. Do it once more and breathe in as the air fills your lungs. Feel how relaxing the sensation is in your body and allow the air to capture any stress left over in your thoughts as it leaves your body. Gently open your eyes and feel how much lighter your body feels.

Ten-Minute Session

This is the most common duration for daily practice, and it gives you the full experience. Get into your learned position and let's dive in.

Take a deep breath in and listen to the sound of the air as it passes through your nose and down into your chest. Your lungs expand as you acknowledge the air. Press the air out through your mouth as you notice your bottom making contact with the surface beneath you. The next flow of air into your nose helps you straighten your spine to solidify your grounding to the surface beneath you. Hold the breath in your lungs as you feel the connection to the space above you. Press the air out and feel your stomach and chest fall with the exit. Take one more breath in through your nose and feel your head raise to extend your crown to the skies. You can feel the roots extend from your bottom as the air is gently pressed out again.

Your posture is erect, and there is no blockage around your throat as you take another deep breath in and begin counting the breaths. Feel the air exit your lungs as you count the first exhale. Your chest expands once more as you take in the second breath and hold it for a second. Close your eyes as you reach the third breath. Follow your thoughts to your feet as you tense them for a moment. Release the muscles as you press the air out slowly. Your attention moves to your legs now, and you take in the fifth breath and pull the muscles gently. Hold for a second and press the air out as you feel the tension release with the breath.

Feel the tension rise in your pelvic area as you take another breath and hold it. Release the breath as the tightness in your pelvic region relaxes. The next intake of air brings mild tension into your core region, and you embrace it for a second. Now, release it slowly with the air that exits your body. Move into your arms now as you pull the muscles tight when you breathe in and feel them as you hold. Guide the air out of your mouth as the tension leaves your arms. Your neck begins tensing as you breathe in once more and hold it again. Feel how your chest has expanded with the collection of tension that remained behind and press the air out slowly to relieve all tension. Your body feels lighter, and your muscles are ultimately relaxed.

Keep your eyes closed as you move your attention to your head where the mind resides. Watch the thoughts as they flash by your inner sight at unspeakable speeds. Take a deep breath as you slow them down and grasp one. The thought has taken a physical form, and you can touch it, embrace it, and shape it. This thought has an unpleasant shape and disturbs you. It's the thought that was created from something that bothers you. Something that happened today perhaps. This aspect of your life keeps you awake at night. Watch yourself as you interact with it. Feel the emotions that live within it when you run it through your fingers.

You've acknowledged the problem, and you know how the emotions attached to it feel. But you can feel how pliable the thought is and understand how it can be manipulated. It will take time, and you should visit these problematic aspects more often. Feel the shape change as your fingers are guided by your desires. It doesn't matter what this form is; you can feel your fingers altering the form. Release it back into the stream when you find peace with the new formation you molded.

Listen to your breath again as you begin counting. The fresh air enters your lungs and caresses your walls as it lies there for a second. Press it out gently through your mouth, focus on how calm your mind and body are. Count the second breath as you breathe in and hold it before releasing it. Feel the air tickle your nose as you draw the third breath and contain it for a moment. Your eyelids are opening as the air exits your mouth, and you are back in the physical environment, feeling calmer and safer than ever before.

I know this might be a little longer than ten minutes, but I wanted to give you a session to scan your body before you recognize thoughts and issues. You can keep doing this session daily to take on a new form that needs reshaping.

Advanced Weekly Meditations

Practitioners use longer meditations weekly to do a deeper cleanse and relax. It also advances our mindfulness more and helps us travel further into any troubles in our minds. We reach a profound state of tranquillity, and our minds become silenced easier. I would advise a beginner to add a longer session once a week. I will give you a longer session in a later chapter, as well as a full session at the end of this book, to help you until you can enter the state on your own.

People generally start by doubling their meditation time on a day they have more time. I do long sessions on a Sunday morning and afternoon. Okay, I meditate a lot. You can begin by increasing your duration to 20 minutes and gradually working toward a 30 or 60-minute session. You will tap into abilities you never knew existed, and your mindfulness will extend into extreme heights. Skilled people are inevitably better at the "human being game of life."

Think about Buddhist monks for a moment again and recognize how devout they are to their practice. Ancient scriptures describe sages who would meditate for hours. The Dalai Lama is one man that we can admire in the world of mindfulness. He is 84 years old and still spends five hours daily in mindful states, whether it's prayers, incantations, or meditation (Valentine, 2018). The Tibetan Buddhist remains one of the busiest men in his ripe old age and doesn't allow anything to disrupt his routine.

Don't misunderstand my words, either, because reaching into a prolonged silence is challenging at first. It's something that occurs gradually when you gain more comfort and peace in your mind. The space you enter should become more welcoming with time. The average mindless person is uncomfortable remaining in this silence that is the present time. Our minds are hard-wired to move in the direction of forward, and throwing a pause in the works takes time to hone it to perfection.

Motivation is one way of persuading yourself to remain calm, and it comes from your reason for needing mindfulness. Do you wish to cleanse yourself? Do you want to strengthen your mind? What is your motivation for meditating? I'll go into further details soon so that you can comb through your motivations and set yourself up for success.

The final piece of advice I can give you for longer meditation is to use something to help you focus. You can use mantras during your session and add a mala to it. A mala is a string of beads that you count as you repeat your mantras. Mantras or affirmations will help you lengthen the duration of your stillness. Mantras are specific sounds that have been mastered over centuries and sound like the repetition of vowels. They resonate with a precise sound vibration through your system. For example, "Om" is a mantra. Affirmations are words you choose to speak over yourself. One might be when you keep repeating phrases that boost your self-esteem, such as, "I am a valuable person, and nothing can break me," or "I am a wonderful parent, and I teach my child valuable life skills."

CHAPTER 5:

TURNING MEDITATION INTO A DAILY PRACTICE

Some people will feel overwhelmed at this point, but I assure you that meditation can be taught, and I'll show you how to turn this valuable practice into a daily routine. I'll cover issues relating to the most common reasons why people quit before they reach their inner peace and how to overcome them. There is a simple strategy to apply this new routine to your life without driving you into the anxious lane. This technique can be practiced by the entire family, and you can become mentally stronger together. We'll discuss habits and why they correlate to mindfulness as well.

Common Pitfalls to Avoid

Meditation doesn't come naturally without effort; it's a skill that we must grow. There are far too many people who pass on the technique after a week or two because they don't see improvements yet. There are multiple reasons why they believe it fails. The first one is endurance. Think about a baby and how they learn to walk. How many times does the little one fall on their backside before they manage to catch their rhythm? The same goes for language skills. No baby was ever born able to speak full sentences but blurted their first words in utter cuteness. They commonly start with one-word responses to everything. It's not that they're incapable of talking; it's a common life skill that must be guided and learned over time. They don't automatically know the alphabet when they start school either. They learn to associate animals to each letter of the alphabet before they even learn what the order is. Anyone who expects to shift their mind into a new rhythm in one or two weeks spends their time in a vastly unrealistic world.

The second reason people opt out is that they don't have time. My life is just as busy, and kids don't give us much time to ourselves. This never stopped me from introducing myself to the practice. Let me use a homemaker as an example here, but you can alter the scenario for any profession. I knew my children returned from school at a specific time of the day, and I often found myself pressed for time to get their lunch ready. I once made them a healthy chicken salad before they got home and managed to enter a mindful state while preparing it.

I took the lettuce and tomatoes out of the fridge and focused on the coolness on my skin. My sense of touch was activated when I carried them over to the counter. I listened attentively to the sound of the knife slicing through the crunchiness until I had the desired pieces. I remember the smell that hit my nostrils as I opened the pack of smoked chicken, not to mention the kiss against my taste buds when I sampled a slice. I shifted my sight to the spectacular colors of the bright green lettuce and the redness of the tomatoes as I placed the bowls in front of my children. I used the simple act of preparing a meal to activate my senses and pay attention to what I was doing in the present moment. That's how easy a subtle mindfulness implementation can be.

The third excuse is when people claim that their schedules vary daily. You can't expect to master the technique if it isn't done every day, or mostly every day. There is no such thing as "I'll try it when I have time." Let me give you an example of a study to show you the benefits of practicing meditation daily for a prolonged period. The National Center for Biotechnology Information (NCBI) often publishes scientific studies for public view and clarity. One that caught my attention focused on the results of brief but daily mindfulness intervention on our ability to maintain focus and stop our minds from wandering off (Rahl et al., 2017). One of the studies published showed a phenomenal increase in attention and focus after participants' meditated over four consecutive weeks. Focus increased by 14% and their wandering thoughts decreased by 22%. This should be motivation for getting your kids on board because they need improvement in attention to excel in school and as adults.

I have broken three myths for you. Don't allow excuses to stop your family from reaching its full potential. I'm going to help you establish a daily routine so that you can focus on your practice.

The Daily Routine

The best chance your family has for creating mindful beings is to turn it into a routine, just as you turned your work and running the rest of the home into one. There's no need for drastic changes in the beginning, and meditation won't interfere with your daily tasks. Implement the example I gave you in the previous section when you experience any unexpected detours in your daily schedule so that there will be no more excuses. You can find a way to meditate briefly, no matter how urgent the deviation might be.

Step one of creating your family routine is to choose the duration for mindful sessions. Take it from someone who's able to sit in her silence for more than an hour at a time now; baby steps are the way to go. I never began with ten-minute sessions but designated two minutes at a time for the first week. You are aiming for quality over quantity. Your mind isn't accustomed to the prolonged quiet time and will struggle to adapt to long sessions from the get-go. Introduce your conscious and subconscious minds to brief interventions.

This is another key aspect of setting a new ritual in your life. You're less likely to dread something if it happens in short stints daily. Your mind will head for the hills if you pressure it to conform to your routine for an hour once a week, so two to three two-minute sessions daily is the preferred way. I did a two-minute session every morning for the first week and then moved onto five-minute sessions for the second week. It was only in my third week that I extended the time to ten minutes. It took a month for me to reach the 20-minute sessions. Use a calendar or spreadsheet on your refrigerator where your family can see their tasks for the day.

You don't need to do it as a family, but having support from other people makes it easier. Meditation is falsely seen as a practice that must be exercised on its own, but that isn't the case. Your family is welcome to share the experience, and you can have group sessions and individual sessions. There should be no discussions in the group exercise, and you can sit apart from each other so you can each focus on your breathing alone. Keep in mind that it should be a silent exercise.

Choosing a time for meditation is another necessity. I practice in the morning because my mind is fresh, and it allows me to enter the day mindfully. The time of day doesn't matter, though, and the only rule is that it should suit you. There's another insert you can add to your time. Have you noticed how much easier it is to retain something in your memory when you connect an object or relatable trigger to it? I'll discuss this in habits in the next section, but creating a daily ritual is forming a habit. Choose a trigger situation or even an object to use before every session. Many people love drinking coffee, and you can use this as your spark. Remember to drink a cup of coffee before you sit down in the morning and enter your mindful state. Jot these times down in your spreadsheet routine. I used an entertaining method for this, and the kids loved it. I purchased a stack of smiley stickers and would stick them in the time slots for meditation. Our inner peace is the deeper level of happiness, after all.

The place you choose is the next part of setting a daily routine. Improvisation will come naturally when you master the technique, but try to have a quiet space designated to meditation in your home or even at work. Make sure the place has no distractions. Remove sounds that draw your attention, and even images on the walls. You want to do this in the beginning, but you can expand your meditation spaces to just about anywhere after a few weeks. Go to the beach if you live near the ocean or sit in the park under a tree. The sounds of the waves crashing against the rocks can give you an additional focus point while you reach into your mind. But for starters, begin in a quiet room.

I know I've shared the correct seated posture with you, but comfort is the next part of daily habits. You're more likely to split from your task if you become uncomfortable or your leg cramps up. I advise against lying down because it's easy to fall asleep, but do what makes you comfortable. Some people sit on a chair with their feet resting on the ground beneath them. Their backs are supported, and their arms rest on the armrests. You will be able to reach your subconscious while standing after you've practiced long enough. Wear clothes that don't hinder your comfort and position yourself as best you can while keeping your spine as straight as possible. You can even try the kneeling position for short meditations.

I will encourage you to use guided imagery meditation to begin with. Headspace is a great app that you can download on your phone; they charge a minimal monthly fee, but the first two weeks are free for you to try it. This app allows you to choose from thousands of professionally guided meditations and even keeps track of your progress. It will remind you to meditate, depending on the schedule you set on your phone. You can choose your goals, which can include mindfulness, stress reduction, attention enhancing sessions, and voice-guided exercises to help you sleep. You can find it on the Apple or Samsung Galaxy stores.

YouTube is another endless guide for free sessions. It's important to use recorded exercises to introduce you to the technique to ensure that your motivation doesn't waver. You don't want to doubt yourself like many people who fail at mindfulness. I love the sessions posted on YouTube because they are often accompanied by relaxing background noise, such as waves or rain. Use the world of information available online to prevent any deviations from the schedule. Most practitioners aren't able to paint a mental picture themselves in the first few weeks and rely on meditation guides online. We need to ignite our imaginations again because they've never deserted us; they are only waiting for us to re-activate them.

The final key to remember in your schedule is your breathing; don't allow anything to distract you from this. You can even schedule time daily to practice your breathing on its own so that nothing can interrupt your focus on the technique. Listen to the air pass through your nose and feel the build-up in your lungs.

The Quick Fix

I want to give you another quick fix technique when you deviate, whether it's intentional or not, because I know it's difficult to stick to a new schedule. I call it the laziest form of meditation possible. A mindfulness guru called Shinzen Young is revolutionizing meditation with a technique he calls the "do nothing technique," and I've developed my own version of it. I use it to redirect blame away from myself when I've deviated a few times and to simply let go. Let me teach you about my lazy technique.

Sit in a comfortable position that suits you best. You can even lie down for this one. Listen to your breathing and focus on the rise and fall of your chest as the sound permeates your mind. Close your eyes and keep focusing on the breaths and the movement of your upper body. You can listen to your heartbeats as well and count them slowly until you reach the number ten. Continue breathing this way until your breaths become longer, and the movements themselves become distant. Time is not the essence of this exercise.

The moment you think about time, I want you to kick the thought to the curb. Timing yourself is just a distraction. The thought about the words I just spoke can be shoved in front of a moving bus too. Lie there in stillness and play baseball with any thoughts that try to creep into your quiet space now. Any urge you feel to get up can be slammed for a home run. Stay in this position as long as you like and keep bouncing thoughts, urges, and emotions away from you.

The urge to sleep crawls near, and you stomp on it. The urge to move your arm is tickling your fancy, but you get rid of it. The thought of thinking itself is too exhausting right now, and you just lie there in your creation of serenity. Forget about every task that needs to be done and focus on nothing and nothing alone. See the blank space that pushes the distractions of your mind further away with every breath you take. Keep at it until you have a blank canvas to begin your day with again.

Creating Habits

There's much debate about where the famous phrase began that tells us that old habits die hard. Some people try to credit Jeremy Belknap as being the first person to say it, but who knows. Nevertheless, I love this phrase. Pay attention to the last word: hard. Not once does the phrase mention an impossibility. It describes an action that will be challenging, but it doesn't define a motion that isn't within our grasp. Habits form from the rituals we partake in daily. Some of these habits can be rather negative, and some can be life-promoting.

Habits are merely repetitive behaviors that begin in our lives. They account for 40% of the influence on our decisions and behavior, according to psychologist David Neal and his associates at Duke University (Neal et al., 2011). This also means that our mindfulness can account for 40% of our behavior when we attune it.

Creating a daily meditation ritual is another simple way of forming a habit, and that's why I recognize them as one. Refer back to the motivation for your desire to reach mindfulness through meditation. Humans set their eyes on something they want, and this stirs passion in their minds and hearts. Make sure you know why you want this before you continue with the steps to form a new habit.

The first step is to choose a goal that is small and work your way to bigger things. I've discussed this in choosing the duration of your meditation sessions. You don't want to leap to insurmountable things when you begin and should start with basic sessions as well. Your goals should be attainable; don't expect the impossible from yourself because that's a recipe for failure. You cannot expect to enter a spiritual connection in your first session but will begin with breathing and mindful tactics first. The quick fix technique allows us to set the bar so low that we can't fail. You're not treating yourself as an imbecile but rather someone who is training to be the best they can be.

The second step is increasing your habit in small segments. Do not jump from the basic one-minute meditation to the transcendental meditation. There are numerous steps before you get there. Time is not the only graduation, and you can think of it as your children in school again. They are required to complete one grade before moving onto the next.

The third step is one I used myself. Imagine you're back in school and your teacher has just asked you to solve a complicated math problem. Educators express the need for breaking the sum up into small sections before you plow straight through it. The same applies to any habit you're trying to create. This goes back to using your routine daily rather than once a week because a task seems simpler when it's broken into smaller segments. The day you switch over to ten-minute meditation sessions, feel free to divide them into two five-minute sessions as well. The mountain doesn't look as high once you see the task as tiny fragments of activity.

The fourth step is acknowledging failure and not giving it a chance to define you. It doesn't matter if you missed one day because you had an emergency at work and stayed late. Make yourself a promise that you will never miss two days in a row. Don't beat yourself up, but instead, prepare for failure with something similar to my quick-fix solution or even becoming mindful about your surroundings when you eat a sandwich. Stay on track, no matter what.

The final step to implementing a new habit is to be patient with yourself. Lower your expectations and learn to become mindful at a pace that suits you. My mother used to love telling me that Rome wasn't built in a day; it's hard to be compassionate and patient with myself, though. I expect myself to be able to achieve anything I set my mind to in an unreasonably short amount of time. Don't be this person but show compassion to yourself as well as your family members. One of you might progress faster than the others. This doesn't mean your son is more intelligent than your daughter, or that you are over your partner.

There's a known fact about habit formation. It will come easy in the beginning, and then the hard part comes later. Perseverance is key; just know that the hard period will pass just as everything else in life does.

CHAPTER 6:

HOW TO TRANSITION FROM SPORADIC TO PEACEFUL PARENTING

Meditation alone isn't going to cut it when it comes to a family. I know how chaotic some days can be. The children are all over the place, and the parents become overwhelmed before they know it. I'm going to guide you away from sporadic parenting in this chapter and on to the wonderful world of peaceful parenting I shared with you earlier. I know the transition can appear frightening for a few, but I guarantee you that it's practical when following the seven steps to get there.

The Advantages of Peaceful Parenting

This almost goes back to habitual lifestyles again because our families have a set way of dealing with life and all it hands us. Transitioning to a new parenting style is an obstacle on its own, and it will come with hurdles we need to overcome. This kind of parenting requires us to create new relationship types between our family members, and it's easy to begin doubting when your youngster raises their voice to you. Keep in mind that your children are going through a change with you, and it will take time for them to adapt to their new habits as well. When dealing with older children and teenagers that are raging with hormones, having them lash out at you does not mean you've failed before you began.

Your child is forming new habits themselves, and any inappropriate behavior toward you could just be a reflection of what they assumed reality to be like. Perhaps there were endless arguments in the home, and now, the child is reacting as they remember the family responding to each other. Children who were yelled at frequently or punished tend to be misunderstood, and they feel lonely. Parents need to set the example, and your compassion and kindness will rub off on them if you remain consistent. The only act that can heal past wounds is compassion.

Every family has a history, and it's often partially tainted with mixed communications and hurt feelings. Peaceful parenting helps us recover gradually and become a singular unit again. You should understand the importance of not allowing the past to define your future if mindfulness conveys the right message to you. I'm also not only taking the part of your children because parents can suffer deep distresses too. We blame ourselves for our children turning reckless or wayward, when, in fact, we are focusing on the past. We cannot ruminate about the time we yelled at them for missing their curfew.

Emotional damage is easily established in both adults and children. Undoing the damage is the challenge, and that's why transitioning between parenting styles is tricky. It can be done, and when you all move from erratic behavior to a new benevolent connection, you are well on your way. Time will remove the injuries inflicted on each member of the family that was caused by disputes, stress, and unfortunate events.

I must share something with you because I see it all too often. There are a handful of parents who still use ancient rearing strategies, and the hierarchy in their home is a mess. The father is like the king, and the wife is the messenger who says yes or no to the kids. There's hardly a connection in the family, and the children are to be seen but not heard. They have no voice, and their parents think of them as robotic beings.

Those parents forget that their children are impressionable beings who are filled to the brim with emotions and scars. I know you're not one of those parents, though, because you wouldn't be reading this book if you were.

Seven Steps to Peaceful Parenting

I'm going to walk through the steps you need to implement in your home to slowly shift your parenting from a state of emergency to a peaceful plain. I've introduced you to the three principles of peaceful parenting, and I'll walk you through the changeover now. The cornerstones I've discussed are embedded in here, but there is some additional information for you to acknowledge and implement daily.

Step One: The Peace Within

I cannot emphasize enough the role of parents. Your role should be as a role model—pun intended. We expect our children to grow up as emotionally stable adults, but their highly impressionable minds are constantly taking silent queues from us, whether we intend for this or not. One of the most attractive and successful traits in any person is emotional intelligence. This means that we should be able to regulate our feelings in the face of distress, anger, fear, and even disappointment.

Think back to the example of implementing a subtle form of meditation in your day when you run short of time. This will be difficult in the beginning, but you can use the motivation from seeing your children thrive in adulthood as the passion to practice silence and regulation. Commit yourself to the parental "stop, drop, and roll."

There's no switch to turn our emotions and responses off, but we can use the advantage of stopping dead in our tracks and dropping all that we're busy with temporarily. The duration of this will shorten as you learn to perfect the skill. This works every time unless you're in the middle of something you can't suddenly halt. Please don't frantically pull over four lanes of traffic to stop on the side of the road, because even your child will look at you stunned. That's why I'm referring back to the example of making lunch.

Let's say your child is throwing a major tantrum in the supermarket, and your face is turning blood red. Turn your attention to your breathing and listen to the sound of air passing through your respiratory tract. Breathe deeply three times and look around you to identify five objects. What can you see? What can you hear? What can you smell? What can you feel? Finally, what can you taste in your mouth? The last one might not always be possible, but you may have a lingering taste of toothpaste or food.

Use your five senses to bring yourself back to the present before you erupt like Pompeii. This happens fast and jerks you back to here and now so that your brain can process information and feelings quickly to handle the situation without yelling at the top of your lungs. It prevents us from reacting in a way we regret, and our children are not scorned with a reprimand.

I want to share a fun science fact with you before we move on. Self-control is an innate skill we all have, and certain practices can improve it dramatically (Self-Control, n.d.). Our ability to regulate our impulses reside in our prefrontal cortex, and this is how we solve problems, regulate emotions, and choose our responsive behavior. Activating and training this part of the brain can lead to a volume increase in your gray matter. Yes, we can grow the size of our brains. Emotional regulation is another skill we need to learn, and if we can change the size of our brains, why can't we change the content of it?

Step Two: Familial Connections

Connecting with your children is another topic I've brushed before, but I'll expand a little further now. Let me tell you once more that peaceful parenting isn't possible if you don't have a bond with your child. It will complicate matters if you simply drop punishment from the table because your child still won't have the motivation required to do the right thing. They'll see you as a pushover who's gone soft and take advantage of you every chance they get.

The first thing you do is dedicate 15 minutes a day with each child. This time is for the two of you, and you can do anything. Small children love bedtime stories, and you can create a nighttime ritual in which you act out the scenes from their favorite storybook. Spend time doing what they love and keep a close physical bond. Don't forget their goodnight kisses and tuck them in comfortably. Teenagers can be more complicated, but you can get involved in their hobbies and support them.

You can explain what's happening once you've established a considerable bond. Sit them down and speak to them about the changes taking place. Ask them if they've noticed that you yell less now, and welcome them on board to the new family plan. Make them feel appreciated and acknowledged by asking them straight out for their cooperation. This might take more than one try.

Step Three: Win-Win Strategies

Everybody loves to win, and we all deserve some extent of it. Children are competitive, and they pick up signals easier than us. Let's use an example of two brothers arguing day and night, because boys will be boys. You need to find out why they're disagreeing and avoid any bias whatsoever. The two boys are sharing a room, and a computer, to top it off. How does one create a win-win situation here? The arguments are mostly about computer usage and both of the boys have needs.

Sit down with them and ask them to help you create a schedule in which each child uses the computer. Look at homework as one aspect because they will need to do some research. The boys love gaming, but they are interested in different games. Shall they get equal time every day to spend on their leisure activities? You can even speak to a tech guy and find out about split-screen options and buy one more set of headphones and controllers. Be sure to involve them in the solution because you want both boys to feel like they've won.

Parents should always acknowledge each child's feelings during this conflict, as well. You can split them up and explain to them how their feelings are valuable. You know your older son is upset because he has twice as much homework, but his little brother wants the same amount of work time on the computer. Recognize his feelings by asking him to help you find a solution that will suit both of them because you know how older siblings can be annoyed by younger siblings.

It doesn't matter what the dispute is about; you need to find a solution that benefits both parties involved. This applies to a disagreement between yourself and your child as well.

Step Four: Limitations

Punishment is off the table, so how do you discipline your child? This will only work if you've created a bond of trust between you. You've had that conversation in which you discussed the new strategy in your home, and there's no need to change the rules. The previous step, combined with compassion, allows you to see your child's point of view now, and that's a good thing. A family is a unity of people who work together, and there's no need for one person to be miserable to make everyone else happy. However, limits are the only way you discipline your child now.

The bond you created has given them the motivation to want to do what's right. People also tend to return kindness when they receive it. Now, you can implement psychology to help you keep these limits. Show your child how much you respect and acknowledge their perception of a situation, and this will make cooperation easier. You want to set the limit before you burst into anger and are still able to use compassion and humor.

Bedtime is a limit, and you can practice empathy by telling your child, "I know you'd love to play more, but you won't have the energy to play tomorrow if you burn it all up tonight." You have seen and acknowledged their desire to continue playtime before you reminded them of the rule of bedtime. Limits play a huge role in discipline, and if you've followed the steps thus far, your child is more likely to collaborate with you.

Step Five: Reparation

This relates strongly to old habits again because a job will feel unfinished if you let something go that would normally be punished. Another new habit for the collection you've gathered so far is to learn to repair rather than punish. It will also give you closure on a situation and avoid leaving you feeling incomplete. I suppose in those terms, this one is for the parents' benefit.

No child can be expected to live life without breaking a rule from time to time. They all have that little ounce of rebellion in them. Sometimes, it can be unintentional as well. Emotions will rise, and you can use your strategy to calm yourself down before you have a private discussion with them. Dig deep to conjure up your patience, and listen to your child. Open the discussion with empathy as you tell them, "I know you were upset when he did that to you."

Give your child the floor to speak before you interrupt them so that they can share all the details with you. Gently point out the consequences of their reaction without applying blame to them. Explain how it hurt their brother's feelings when they yelled at him. Their little brother might fear them now and feel distant. Now comes the important part because you shouldn't tell your child *how* to repair the damage.

Ask your child how they think it can be repaired. You are not forcing an apology. This responsibility you hand to your child will empower them when they're free to correct things themselves. Talk about a relationship struggle you might have had with a friend and how you repaired it. Try and inspire them to do the right thing without actually instructing them. They will relish their own make-up with their sibling when they decide how to do it.

There can be resistance from your child, and this is when you need to help heal from their pains further. Make sure that you are speaking from an example and seeing things from their viewpoint. Look out for any warning signs of an age-old wound that was created between the siblings in the previous parenting style and begin working on recovery.

Step Six: Dealing with Emotions

Emotions are inevitable, but you can respond differently. Children are developing automatic responses, and every time a "bad" emotion gets them into hot water, they learn from this and begin suppressing their feelings instead. Accumulating emotions is the worst thing possible because your child will explode when they're provoked at the wrong time. Punishment is the reason kids repress their feelings because they become afraid of showing them.

The day your child blows their top is when all these hidden emotions surface, and they don't know how to express them in words. Fear brewed inside them every time you yelled at your child, and it remains present in their minds. Their automatic response to fear is acting out because they're afraid of punishment if they show their feelings.

It will take plenty of connection time to overcome this. Watch a sad movie with your child and never tell them they aren't allowed to cry. Allow your tears to flow with theirs. I knew a man who used to tell his son that it was inappropriate to laugh alone. He would refer to "crazy" people who laugh for no reason. I disliked this man very much because children laugh, and it gets that feel-good chemical called dopamine running through their veins. Laughing together is an excellent way to bond. The bottom line is that you should encourage your child to show their emotions without judgment.

Besides creating an emotionally friendly environment, you can encourage good behavior with appreciation. Tell your child how proud you are that they handled the situation correctly. Explain how it pulled your heartstrings when you saw their reaction to the homeless man. Make your child want to repeat their behavior by giving them recognition and appreciation for it.

Step Seven: The Safety Net

Parents are supposed to be the safety net for their children when they go through life's traumas. Adulthood doesn't make us immune to distress, and even we still need someone to be our shoulder to cry on. I want my children to feel as though they can tell me anything, even when they're 50-years-old. There's one trick to this, though, and it goes back to your emotional regulation. You need to react to something your child tells you and remain calm. The moment you respond aggressively or out of disappointment, you break the bond you've worked so hard to create.

Think of it as walking on thin ice. Children experience trauma differently than us, and they might not have the coping mechanisms that we do. They can break down and sink into a hole of depression or anxiety. Continue expressing compassion and wait until your child opens up to you. You might be able to see the surface of the scar, but you can't always see what caused it.

Children often turn to anger to cope with their fears or insecurities that formed from past wounds. It doesn't matter how mad they get, you stay tranquil and wait for them to share with you. Anger cries have a healing effect on their own. Haven't you noticed how much better you feel after a good cry? Encourage the flow of tears so that they can release those hurtful emotions inside of them.

My final advice in this chapter is that you commit to changes every day, just as you established a routine for meditation. Wake up in the morning and smile because you know that you're going to implement these changes even further each day.

CHAPTER 7:

THE PRESENT MOMENT

Living in the present moment has been embraced throughout this book, but it is one of the most powerful tactics of mindfulness. It allows us to view the world realistically and remove any delusions people commonly suffer from. There are countless advantages of living presently for you and your family. Moments that seemed insurmountable will become mere hurdles that you leap over gracefully. Our lives become new, and we learn to cope with some of the most difficult aches that frequent human nature. Some of these pains are deeply embedded in our spirits. I'm going to reveal the in-depth details of the present moment and give you the tools to eradicate the problems for good.

Introductions and Formalities

I know you have a broader understanding of the concept by now, but I want to expand your knowledge base to a whole new level. Spiritualism comes into play here because its deeper connection lies within it. I am not talking of one god or another but an association to something higher than us because this can provide stability and understanding in our lives. Bringing ourselves to the present can help us understand our true nature, and it's the only entry point for time itself.

Time and the now are intertwined like the words of a sentence need to blend for us to understand it. One cannot exist without the other. I've spent time on time itself, but it's related to a broader spectrum of definitions. Time is merely an illusion that distracts us from the present. The only place it can exist is now. We cannot touch, see, smell, hear, or feel the time that existed yesterday because there's no reality in it. Yesterday is a compilation of memory fragments in our brains, but it's not something we can touch or experience presently in any way.

Tomorrow is another object that doesn't exist anywhere but in our minds. Our brain and the neurons in it are endlessly puzzling together fragments of memory to create a projection of tomorrow. Let's use a simple example here. Look at the time on your watch now and close your eyes. I want you to count to 60 in your present time and look down at your watch again. Guess what? Time still only exists now. One minute before you looked down and one minute from now is a figment of our imagination. The space-time continuum no longer exists, and there is no reality in the fabric of one minute ago.

Time has a physical form of some kind right now. It is the restructuring of forms in front of you at this very moment. The world never stops turning, and neither does it end the cycle around the sun. Time is merely a perception of movement and can only be seen right now. Even the memories in your brain are constantly reshaping themselves as "time" moves on. Time is a delusion that we all suffer from, and it only exists now.

The past and future continue along a horizontal timeline, and you need to exit this to see the vertical line that connects them. The present moment resides in that vertical line. Mahatma Gandhi once said, "The future depends on what we do in the present." Our opportunities burst wide open when we find the vertical line. Goal-setting is incredibly important, but it requires us to set in motion any changes we need in the present moment. The quality of what we do now will determine the outcome of the future.

The Time Captor

The delusional existence that contains no reality isn't afraid of taking prisoners. Your mind and spirit are captured in the past or future, and in some cases, both. This, unfortunately, allows thoughts to control you because your mind reminds you of what happened or what's to come. This can be useful in some instances when your mind recognizes a threat that you encountered before, and self-preservation kicks into overdrive. Daydreams of future improvement are most welcome too, because they give us the motivation to be the person we wish to be.

Our captors can prevent us from seeing the present when they persistently bombard our minds with thoughts and emotions from past events or future concerns. Depression can creep up on us when we can't shake the traumatic memory of losing a loved one. Anxiety is the face of future fear because we concern ourselves with potential failure instead of doing something about it now. You are doing something by learning how to break the shackles, but so many people fear that their children will grow up to be vandals and poverty-stricken couch potatoes.

Our awareness of the here and now fades away, and we struggle to find happiness in our lives. This is when a systematic negativity grabs hold, and bad habits start to form. Our behaviors can be erratic, and we latch onto the infamous corruptions available to us. There's one way to permanently shake the grounds of this mental abductor. You are aware that time is a delusion now, and how can an illusion keep you prisoner? It is just a name we gave it as humans, and mother nature doesn't recognize it at all.

You can touch "time" in the present by touching an object in front of you right now. The sensors on your fingertips can't feel an object yesterday. The same applies to emotions because we can't receive abundant contentment unless we sever the cord around our necks and take time as a prisoner ourselves. You control it, and you decide what shape to form. It's no wonder society has become depressed and anxious, fighting off stress like fast-spreading cancer. It's because we allow this feeble-minded character to pull the wool over our eyes.

Do you want to rid yourself of the burdens we call stress, anxiety, and depression? Then make a stand now and promise yourself that this imaginary creature won't rule the roost anymore.

Taking Charge

You've learned about handling your children's emotions, but what about your own? You also have pain inside, and just because you took back the reins doesn't make it disappear. Emotions come from memories that develop thoughts. Taking back the steering wheel doesn't magically instruct them to expire. You understand that all you have left in the present is a collection of one-time moments. Those moments will be connected to past pains and experiences. Use this moment to expose yourself to deeper troubles that cause you discord.

Allow these thoughts and feelings to enter your present space so that you can deal with them. A child shouldn't repress emotions, and neither should you. Spend time with feelings that surface at the moment and acknowledge them for what they are. You don't even need to interrupt them because they are simply illusions from past experiences.

Show compassion for these feelings rather than shoving them aside. Think about your kids again and how they often seek attention. Your emotions are similar to children, and they want to be heard and noticed. Give them the pleasure of recognition and watch as they pass like a child who got the attention they yearned for. The greatest gain we can receive from living in the now is when our minds are freed from all the troubled thoughts that once hid away.

Tips to Master Present Living

I've compiled the best efforts in practicing this necessary skill for you. I use these methods myself, and they've saved me from slipping back into the clutches of time again. Many people believe that we can come back to the present by thinking about it alone, and this is, sadly, a misconception. Some of the tips I'll share with you can be practiced daily, and there's no need to wait for time to pop its hideous head out.

Crisis Control

Breathing is one technique I've introduced to you many times. Nothing speaks like the sound of air passing through your lungs and down into your stomach as it rises. The beauty is that breathing is a natural process that remains with us until the day we draw our last breath. It's available at any given moment in any situation. Imagine yourself in an important business meeting, and your spouse calls. You press the phone to ignore it the first time, but then they call again. The two of you agreed that the second call indicates an emergency.

You can already feel your chest tighten as you look over at your client, and the words escape your mouth. "I'm sorry, but I have to take this call." Your heart is beating through your shirt, and all kinds of thoughts slip into your mind. You're not sure what concerns you more. The fact that an emergency call is coming or you have to interrupt a meeting with a client that determines the future of your business.

There's only one immediate go-to method in this instance, and that's breathing deeply. You answer the phone, and your spouse is frantic because your son was injured at his football game. He is being rushed to the emergency room as you speak. This has ignited a vicious mixture of emotions in you, and you have lost track of "time." Take deep breaths in and out as you feel your stomach welcome the fresh air. Feel free to smile slightly when your client looks over at you and keep breathing. This is considered the crisis response to a sudden disruption in your timeline.

Bodily Focus

Another fast reaction to time disruption is scanning your body consciously. This includes the internal and external aspects of it. The man sitting across from his client can use a combination of the two techniques without looking like a frenzied zombie. He can notice how his hand feels against the mobile phone, and the other hand that's touching the droplets of water on the glass. He can focus on his feet and feel how they connect to the ground below. The air is physically embracing his lungs, and he can visualize them expanding as his heart is pumping blood to his extremities.

He pays attention to the way his tongue moves as he inhales, and he can even picture the expression on his face. Bringing attention to his body as it sits in that chair right now will empower him to control time again. Remember that your body can only exist in the present. I wouldn't suggest that this man move his hands up and down his body as he sits with a future associate, but I would advise this if you're alone.

Move your hands from your face down to the furthest reach on your body. I use this myself, and the friction between my fingers and the tiny sensors along my skin is a great way to nudge myself back. The movements also remind me how I'm able to conform time to my will and desire.

Raising the White Flag

This is one way you can control something that seems to be in chaos. I've mentioned how important emotional exposure and acceptance is in this journey. Now I'll elaborate with an example you can use at the moment.

The second this man's spouse explained that his son was injured during the game was the moment his thoughts ran wild. He played football himself, and he remembers the day that he ended his hobby. It wasn't an injury he suffered himself but rather one that befell a teammate. The quarterback was plowing down the field to score a touchdown when a larger boy came out of nowhere and smashed into him. The young quarterback's dreams were shattered when his skull shattered the poles. The boy suffered traumatic brain injuries and became a shell of his former self. This businessman can recall a couple of years ago when he saw how brain-damaged his former teammate was at the 20-year reunion. The man still lives with his mom because he is unable to look after himself.

This is massively tragic, and we can all imagine the emotions steaming through the businessman's mind when he allowed his thoughts to consume him. Time took advantage and shackled him in prison again. How do we expect this man to suppress those horrid emotions and memories? He is suffering from a terrifying fear of what is to come. How will his son look when he gets to the hospital? His spouse is hysterical and can't express words in an understandable tone.

All the man can do at this moment is embrace the emotions. He should sit there while breathing and noticing his body while he welcomes feelings of dread into his body. He allows his mind to wander into the memories and the nightmarish projections of the future. His focus shifts, and he gives the painful memories a physical form and presence. This requires much attention, and the person might look strange in this setting. However, even the client will understand under the circumstances.

I would close my eyes in this scenario and listen to my breath as I feel myself up. That pain has formed a physical object in my chest now. It hurts, but I don't interfere with it. I surrender without judgment because I'm allowed to feel this throbbing ache in my chest. I will move my hand to my chest area so that there can be a connection between the pain inside and physical movement. I'm shaping time once more. I'm empathizing with myself and focusing on the feeling that causes my heart to beat faster.

Allowing it to take on a physical form has given me control over time again, and I can feel the pain subsiding slowly. My thoughts move back to the task at hand now. I would explain the situation to the client and ask that we postpone the meeting. I guarantee you that they will have seen your face go white as you focused on the pain in your chest. Keen observation can bring us back to the here and now.

Controlled Distraction

The only distraction allowed in mindfulness is when you have full control over it. You can bring yourself back to the present by focusing on your environment. You know to use your five senses and see, smell, feel, taste, and hear the objects of your focus. There isn't an object on this earth that you can't use to concentrate on. I'm going to share a personal experience with you as an example here.

I was with a tour group as a younger woman, and I hardly knew the other people. My mindful journey was fairly new, and I was still practicing my chosen methods. We had just arrived at a botanical garden that was famous for housing spectacular fauna and flora. I had made new "friends," but they were practically strangers to me. I was walking alongside a young woman who was telling me about the craziness of her first year at college when my phone rang.

Isn't it funny how most of these stories can begin with a phone ringing? But this is my true story. It was a loved one who phoned to tell me I needed to return from my trip because another loved one had just passed away. I won't go into the details of it, but let's just say it was a horrible and sudden death of someone I would never have expected.

Nevertheless, I was unable to breathe, and I dropped my phone. The young lady with me was jerking my arm and the sound of her voice was distinctly distant and fading further all the time. I was finding it very hard to regulate my breath again, and I couldn't move from where I stood. I had merged with the ground beneath me.

Suddenly, the most unexpected thing happened to me, and this is the very moment I perfected my controlled distraction. The most gorgeous butterfly touched my skin, never mind the woman who was pulling my arm. I shrugged my arm back as the butterfly became glued to me, and my mind stopped being so excessively loud. I looked at the colors and could feel the tiny feet dancing on my skin. I brought my right hand closer and placed my finger in front of the butterfly.

It hopped onto my finger as though I was its best friend. The noises in my head were growing more and more distant, and the sound of this lady shouting for help was becoming clearer. She had run off to find someone who could help me because she was worried and confused. I raised the butterfly in line with my eyes, and as I watched the wings fluttering gently, a tear escaped my eye. All the loudness from my thoughts had dissipated, and the lady was headed back to me with a security guard.

The butterfly flew away, and I crumbled to the ground. I felt the grass beneath me and was finally back in the present, allowing my emotions to flood through me. I've never seen a butterfly like that again, and I still don't know what kind it was. However, this is the technique that saved me instantly from the clutches of time when I focused all my attention on the object that was in front of me. It doesn't need to be a living object, but in this case, it was.

Dreamscapes

The last method seems silly, but it's effective in subtle despair. I must admit that I allowed my mind to wander back to the pain I felt that day in the gardens, but the tears flowing from my eyes tells me that I'm fine in the here and now. I had to do something to ensure that I was fine, though.

Have you ever had a nightmare that seemed utterly unrealistic, but you were terrified anyway? A great way to come out of a dream that disturbs your sleep is to pinch yourself. Yes, you heard that correctly. Giving yourself a quick pain sensation can shift your attention back to the present, and that's why we pinch ourselves when we think we're dreaming. Just please don't pinch yourself too hard. Use this method to return to reality from a nightmare, daydream, or an emotional train of thought.

CHAPTER 8:

CONNECTING IS THE SECRET TO PEACEFUL PARENTING

Connecting with our children can be a challenge in itself, and some of us think we already have the best relationship with them. That's why I've dedicated this chapter to parents who have rocky relationships with their children and need to improve them. The same advice can be applied proficiently to forming new bonds and strengthening old ones. The fact remains that peaceful parenting will be a fruitless effort without that deep connection. Spending time with your children and listening to them is one thing, but you need to master the art of being someone they call a friend and a parent without losing that mutual respect. Life has become complicated for kids, and the days of running free in the streets until the streetlights burn are long gone. They have their own mountain of stress, whether it's homework or personal relationships with their friends. Let's get into it and work toward the relationship both of you deserve.

Renewal and Sustenance

Nothing is carved in stone until you have that union of friendship combined with parenting. Have you noticed how children are open with their friends, and they seek advice, as well as share secrets with them? Take a moment and imagine this with your eyes closed.

Having this kind of relationship with your child will help you enter the friend zone, where they trust you, and disputes can finally move into discussions. Unfortunately, many homes are in constant conflict with each other. These varied phases of war and peace are the reason connecting to your child matters. This union can repair disputes or repressed feelings of anger and repair severed relationships, even when the parent isn't aware of them yet. Future differences will appear insignificant when you and your child are at peace with each other.

Have you ever heard someone say that respect should be earned? Many conflicts in families arise when one party doesn't consider the feelings of another. Parents believe that children have little decision-making power in the home. I've referred to this previously when I spoke of the man who persistently told his children to shush. Every family member's feelings and needs must be taken into account.

The average household experiences multiple mini wars every day, with varying outcomes. Children are human, after all, and when we think they should be happy 24/7, we're dead wrong. One of the first things you should do as a parent is maintain a collected nature, especially when the source of disruption is external. Don't arrive at home with the weight of the world's anger on your shoulders because your day turned out terrible. You will damage your child's trust the moment you explode at them for outside reasons. Their self-esteem, ability to relate to others, and their openness and honesty toward you will suffer.

Nevertheless, you are also human, and conflict can arise from matters that aren't in the home at all. People walk around moody and take their emotions out on their loved ones. It happens, and anyone who denies this is living a lie. The difference is that the eruption must be handled suitably. Children are often silenced in this scenario, and that's a mistake. They should be given the freedom to convey their message and voice their grievances. Never cut your child off when they express themselves in retaliation. There are various ways to repair a dispute, no matter how significant it was.

Your family will begin healing, and there will be a mutual

understanding. After a few reparations, the children will know that repair is possible. They will also trust to be heard and acknowledge their right to express their emotions. They also learn that they are their own person and are allowed to disagree. Problem-solving skills are developed when they know conflicts can be resolved, and this will stay with them in adulthood. Stress will become a productive tool when issues are discussed, and the table remains open for emotions in both directions. You are teaching your children to resolve matters that cause them stress, and they will thrive in life.

Let me give you a few examples to apply during a dispute.

The first thing you want to avoid is giving a kid mixed signals. I'm sure you want to apologize when you took your work anger out on them, but it doesn't help to do this while you're still carrying the rage monster inside of you. Calm down entirely before you apologize to your child, or they will see your remaining emotions and become confused by your actions.

There's one word I want you to forget as a parent, and that monstrosity is the word "but." Never tell your child, "I'm so sorry, *but* you kept asking me when dinner will be ready, and I'm exhausted." This translates to, "I'm kind of sorry, but it was entirely your fault that I exploded." Can you see how this word contradicts an apology?

Another piece of advice is to see your child's apology as a sincere one. It is a tough decision to make when we recognize our faults, and apologizing is hard. You know this very well. Don't retaliate and tell your child, "You say sorry now, but you'll be back at it tomorrow." You are deflecting their sincerity and hurting their feelings. Why don't you just tell them you don't trust them?

You're allowed to be angry yourself. Both of you are entitled to your feelings. There will come a time when you don't see repair yet, and the best thing you can do is exit the room and enter a mindful state. You can even cry too. I did this a few times when my children hurt me. Crying is a wonderful way to express your emotions.

The same applies to your kids, and they might need some space to reflect on the situation. Allow them to take a moment to compose themselves, or you can even encourage them to voice their feelings at you. Don't mockingly do this, but tell them, "I'm sorry for shouting at you. Why don't you express your anger in your loud voice back at me?" Yelling is, unfortunately, a comfort just as crying is, and we all need it once in a while. As long as it's directed at something other than our loved ones.

The final tip I can share is hugging. Spend a minute in a soft embrace with your child when you're done repairing the argument. Don't forget to remind them that you love them every day through actions.

Keep in mind that we are unable to think logically when our emotions are running haywire. Give your kid the time they need to bring their minds back to the present. This parental strategy will equip them for life, and they'll be great problem-solvers.

Stop Yelling!

According to psychologists Laura Markham and Robyn Silverman, yelling at your children is the number one stressor in their lives (Silverman & Markham, 2017). The constant surge of energy exchange adds to the stress parents face as well. Our tongues are like daggers, and the stab from them can make up for most of our relationship problems. Children become fearful of their parents and react as most human beings would. The damage we cause is on an emotional level that runs deep within their minds. The problem is that we frequently believe that we are superior and have strong authority over them. Both of these debates are harmful and false.

Not one of us can reside within our peace every moment of every day. It doesn't matter how hard we try; we will be tested. Here's an interesting point to consider. We are only capable of giving what we have inside ourselves. Children automatically look for the person who will teach them everything, and if you're always yelling, so will they. They can feel our stress and become vulnerable themselves.

Replace frustration with love when you feel like yelling. Keep using your mindful techniques to reach your inner peace so that there will be fewer triggers. Anger is an essential tool that can be used to our advantage instead of destroying our loved ones. Show your child how they should manage their anger. Aggravation can also keep us tethered to disconnection, and you should apply bonding rituals daily to avoid disruption from this emotion.

I've told you about watching funny videos, and this is immensely useful. Laughter releases dopamine, and this chemical induces happiness. You can even watch funny kitten videos online or read the funniest joke compilations. Interrupt rage and other emotions by forcing laughter.

Learn to respond to your child without emotions unless you're showing them unconditional love. Many parents dismiss their feelings and those of their children. This is wrong because we need to validate emotions to live fruitful and mindful lives. These little emotion disruptors can help your child spend more time in a cheerful state rather than an angry, hurting phase, and they'll grow older to relate to positive emotions naturally. This won't happen before your home becomes a peaceful state, and I'm sure you want your child to be a healthy emotional individual.

Essential Modelling

A child's brain isn't fully developed yet; it continues to advance over the years. This is why they are susceptible to great emotions, and this overwhelming avalanche can lead to inappropriate behavior, aggression, rebellion, defiance, and absolute hysteria. The problem is that parents often receive a response and reflect a similar outcome. I can tell you from experience that the worst thing you can say to a child experiencing a meltdown is to shut up. The same goes for people who tell you to calm down when you're upset. I've seen some tragic reactions from people who've been told to calm down. The exact opposite happens, and you

74

can feel the ice in your body when they stare at you. I don't blame someone who runs in this instance. Parents who do this need to spend some time focusing on themselves because telling their kids to calm down will only escalate the situation exponentially.

I'm going to use fear as an example here because I covered anger so many times. Let's talk about ourselves because our children are picking up on our vibes. The environment is everything that surrounds us, and this acts as a trigger. Our senses pick up on queues that stimulate memories and turn into thoughts. Our mind then expels emotions.

Sarah is our subject, and she has been instructed to advance her knowledge to carry on with her career. It's a two-year program and involves chemical engineering. Sarah has a young daughter in middle school and is delighted to find out how much time she can spend at home while studying. Her excitement is bubbling over, and she sits down in front of the computer to examine the material she needs to study.

Suddenly, Sarah lets out a cry, and Sarah's daughter comes running to her aid. She finds her mother in tears, with the bright reflection of light from the screen in front of her. Sarah's daughter tries to console her mother, but her mother is frantic and can barely utter words. After an hour of distorted reaction and talking about failure, Sarah calms down enough to expand on why she fell apart like that.

The fact is that Sarah exploded with fear when her emotions were riled up from the screen in front of her. She became anxious, and a chemical called cortisol was released in her system, sending her into a fight, flight, or freeze moment. Sarah had a complete meltdown due to her fear. The material looks Greek to her, and she spent an hour telling her impressionable daughter about how she would fail the exams and lose her job. The problem is that she reacted inappropriately to her emotion in front of her young girl. Sarah forgot all about mindfulness and dealing with emotions correctly. All she did was instigate the same pattern of emotional regulation in her daughter. How is this child in middle school supposed to react to new tasks, homework, and exams now? She has lost all trust in Sarah's abilities too, and Sarah can't expect her daughter to look up to her anymore in this respect.

Children look up to their parents; that's why they learn from us. It's up to us to give them every reason to believe that they can compose themselves and embrace their fear without a wild response. The behavioral patterns in your brain are deeply set, and you will have to work hard to overcome them and not hand your dysfunctional core beliefs onto your children.

Sarah could have acted differently and brought herself back to the present, breathed deeply, and even took some silent time to ponder the material before she exploded. It's our duty as parents to practice alternatives every chance we get because our kids are always watching. Our lives don't need to be dramatic. Emotional regulation demands a connection between ourselves and our feelings. Spend time finding yourself, connecting with yourself, and then you can connect on an emotional level with your children.

Reinforced Connection Tips

There are a couple of tips I can share with you about reinforcing and strengthening a bond with your children. This will help in reparation and establishment as well.

Empathy

One way of showing your child empathy is to remove the juggle of reward and punishment from their lives. Act as their coach rather than their judge and jury. You will be coaching them from the day you perfect your role model skills. Becoming a composed and non-reactive parent is the only way to break through a potentially difficult relationship.

Equality

Practice equality in your home and make sure your kids know that adults are not superior to children. Their opinions matter and their size makes no difference. You can go down on your knees with small children so that they are not intimidated by your stature. Speak to them while making gentle eye contact. You can place your hand on their shoulder while you speak to create a physical bond while discussing something of importance. This lets them know that you love them even though the topic might be serious. Another strategy I had was to pick them up and stand them on a chair when we discussed matters of concern. You surely don't want a child to feel like they're David, with Goliath hovering over them. They are more open to suggestion and sharing when you "stoop to their level."

I would remember to keep my language empathetic so that they would know I wasn't scolding them. Speak with kindness and tell them, "Your friend at kindergarten was blocking your way, so you pushed him. Pushing him hurts, and you can ask him to step aside instead." It's not just the words you choose but also the tone of your voice.

Limitations

This is merely a reminder to see things from their perspective because every household needs direction, and children who feel understood will abide by the limitations you set. You can tell your child, "I know you're very angry right now, but we needn't bite our sister. Why don't we use our words to express our anger to our sister?" You can apply this to teenagers too. Tell your teenage daughter, "I know the boy hurt your feelings, but we don't scratch other people's cars. Why don't you send him a text and tell him how much he hurt you?"

Safety

Safety carries another face here. There will be situations that need immediate intervention because sibling rivalry is a real thing. I don't need to tell you that. Children can fall prey to their emotions easily and harm one another in anger. This is a clear indication that peaceful parenting is required.

Be careful not to jump in the middle and impose a violent response to break them up. This will not help your cause. Use words and calm tones to break them up. Use words like, "The rule is no physical altercations in this home." This isn't directed at either individually and doesn't assert blame. It's important to get the two of them talking about their emotions as soon as they calm down enough. Allow them to share their anger because they might see it from the other's point of view.

Let's discuss something more serious now. Some children are battling feelings that we don't often see until it's too late. Our lack of connection is to blame for this. You walk in on your teenage child who is about to harm themselves. Avoid any words like "What the hell are you doing?" and "Stop that immediately." Find your peaceful tone of voice and say, "This is a loving home, and we don't harm ourselves. Please speak to me about what you're feeling right now. I am all ears, and my love remains unconditional."

This is a situation I don't wish upon my worst enemy, but it does happen. Use all the skills you've learned in this book so far to help your child come to the present moment. Avoid any words that reinforce the pain they're feeling, and don't make it about yourself. Avoid sentences like, "You're hurting me." Everything is about the connection between you, and nothing else matters in this instance.

Timeouts

Here's some simple advice. Avoid timeouts at all costs because they humiliate your child, stir power struggles, remain a punishment, and only work while you are bigger than your child. Leaving your child to their own thoughts in a corner can harm the connection you're trying to build. I will introduce you to a better form of guidance, or correction, in the next chapter.

CHAPTER 9:

THE CHAIR OF DISPUTES

Not every war in the world has been resolved with the same solution, and sometimes, negotiations need to take place multiple times. We need space to clear our minds before each negotiation. The fact that we're all unique makes peaceful living difficult. I'm going to teach you about a valuable trick to bridge the gap between negotiations without using punishment, reward, or even conflict itself.

The Chair of Disputes Revealed

It doesn't matter how you've integrated mindfulness and peaceful parenting in your home because you and your family will knock heads at some point. Peace can erupt into chaos within seconds, faster than we can imagine. I've found a viable solution to this problem, and I'll emphasize the fact that it's not a timeout. Timeouts are linked to misbehaving toddlers, but this is something next level. It carries numerous benefits besides the idea of calming the storm.

I've often described my idea to fellow parents, and some have looked at me horrified before I could explain what it was in detail. They jump on their high horse and assume it's some form of timeout. I had one lady ask me if I watched *Game of Thrones*. My curiosity got the better of me, and I am highly offended that she would correlate my concept to such a violent series. At least I know she never understood a word I spoke. I've chosen the name because it describes what I see and not some throne that people constantly wage wars over. My chair is one that is meant to discourage and pacify a dispute before it happens. It can also provide time or space between attacks. So, please be patient and recognize the value of this new golden house rule.

I call it the chair of disputes. I took a comfortable chair and placed it in a room in the house that was free from distractions. The chair needs to be isolated and present a peaceful center. I used this chair as a new rule in our home, and whenever one of us became anxious, stressed, emotional, or ready to attack another family member, we would spend a few minutes in the chair. This was a rule for each one of us, not only the children. Chances are, 99% of disputes will be resolved after sitting in the silence of a peaceful space for a while. It was also at this stage I introduced my children to meditation when I placed a speaker in the room where they could listen to serene sounds or brief segments of guided meditation.

The important thing is that the person must be comfortable in that chair. That's why I sneakily used a recliner. If my child felt their emotions boiling when their sibling upset them, they could retreat to their safe place out of their own free will. It was quite a challenge to convince them from the start, but they never saw this as a punishment because who wouldn't mind a ten-minute break in complete silence in a comfortable seat?

Let me explain where the idea came from. I'm sure you're well aware of our emotions driving our anger and aggressive responses. The chair gives us the peace to reflect on our emotions where we are away from unwanted distractions. Believe it or not, the idea began in a hair salon (Anderson, 2017). Hair salons are famous for small talk, and the stylists are usually pressured to establish a conversation with their clients. Bauhaus is a large chain of hairstylists in the United Kingdom, and they began noticing a gap in their industry. Let's face it, the world is filled with anxious people because our emotions can surface at any given time. Bauhaus experimented with a new concept called the "quiet chair."

There was much backlash from the public because salons are known for social interaction, and some people couldn't fathom the idea of silence in a social environment. The chain of salons paid no attention and continued their ambition to welcome clients who suffer from anxiety, depression, post-traumatic stress disorder, and social anxiety into a safe space they'd provided. This didn't only provide relief to the stylists, who never had to chat anymore, but it also boosted business for them because there are so many people who have to take a Xanax just to cut their hair. Fox Den Salons in Minneapolis introduced the idea to the United States, and it took off. Do yourself a favor and visit one of these silent chairs to realize how peaceful the experience can be.

The point I'm making is that the person who sits in the chair of disputes doesn't only calm down and acknowledge their emotions; they also get the chance to just be. It can be horrendous when people keep nagging at us, and we feel down or upset. Mindfulness alone has taught me how valuable my spatial peace can be, and this chair will show your family the benefits. You can add music as I did and provide some headphones so that the person can listen to something that brings a deep sense of calm over their bodies.

Tying Quiet Time to Peace

Quiet time is what forms the base of peace in ourselves and our environment. It is suggested that you don't postpone this healing practice but act on it immediately. Ten minutes in this space can help you come back to the present moment and relieve stress and anxiety. You don't even need to meditate. This sudden interruption of bothersome thoughts and emotions will get you back on track for work, school, and living serenely with your loved ones.

Let's take a look at the benefits of experiencing quiet time in our lives.

The first advantage of this ritual relates profoundly to our emotional wellbeing. Our minds are utterly consumed by thoughts, memories, and emotions when we get upset. No person is immune to the devastating consequences of depression and anxiety. It is something that consumes our joy, our ability to function, and even our ability to reason. We don't want to walk into a disagreement with our motors firing on all cylinders from the start. It's not only about disputes because we have the space to cry when we are hurting, mentally scream when we are angry, and try to make sense of the situation that triggered us in the first place.

Some people used to think I was crazy when I gave myself a "healthy timeout" in public. I remember being so angry that I needed to scream, and so I did. The pressure of the air moving out of my system instantly relieved the immense stress I was under; however, the faces that were staring at me in shock told me that I needed a quiet space. A quiet space doesn't mean I have to remain silent, and I was able to voice my words so that my ears could hear them. I have, on one occasion, shouted in my chair of disputes. There's no judgment or rules in this chair, and my entire family knows this. We know that we go into that room to deal with something emotional before it becomes the family's problem.

The second advantage is that we sometimes want to be alone. I've learned well enough to be alone and happy. It's disturbing to be surrounded by people, family or not, when you reflect on your day honestly and recognize the reasons for your anger. I know that a long, difficult day drains me of all my energy, and the chair rejuvenates my mind, as well as my physical body. We all need rest, and our bodies were never made to run on autopilot all the time. I have no problem taking a break when I feel exhausted. I know I can never switch my thought processes off, but sitting back in that comfortable relaxation allows me to watch them drift past me like leaves on a river. We create a loud noise in our minds when thoughts are left unattended. We need to become aware of them to process the information correctly. I've meditated in this chair for years now, but I've also spent moments of complete silence, and even fallen asleep on a few occasions.

The third advantage I've experienced is when I grew compassionate with myself. The chair helped me do this too. Just the act of sitting there when the world was passing me by, not partaking in the movement itself, is one of the kindest things I've done for myself. Self-compassion is the gateway to the kindness we show our loved ones, and this can help us resolve a counteractive opinion when we see their perspective too.

Another pro is when we are allowed to escape the false reality our thoughts and memories try to impose on us. We can distance ourselves from circumstances beyond our control and remove blame, guilt, and shame from our circles. It's easy to take responsibility for something that isn't ours. Distance provides us with the time we need to realize that it's not our fault. Disputes can't be solved when we want to fix it by wrongly allocating blame to ourselves or others.

Finally, self-reflection in this spatial silence can turn chaos into order. Our problem-solving skills are put to the test when we are overwhelmed. Arguments become heated, and how do we find answers in the heat of the moment? I agree that thoughts travel faster than we can believe, but that is exactly why we must take time to ponder on them. You're able to choose the right thought and the right response when you slow down the thought process through awareness. The longer you take to look at the leaves drifting around, the more time you'll have to choose the response you won't regret. You can also examine each thought and look for reasons why each one is there.

Let me say one final note here. The chair of disputes is not a sanctuary where we sit and wonder how we can win every argument. The idea of being here is to see the argument from every perspective and evaluate all options. Don't use this place to come out with your fists drawn. This is not a military base where wars are strategized in detail. That is not what you're doing here, and this act alone will sever all bonds between family members. Positivity is key, and you need to remember that you're looking for a win-win strategy.

Digging Deeper

There are countless benefits to sitting in the solitude of comfort. I've mentioned how this chair can guide you or family members through disputes and open a new line of communication between you. However, it can be used for more than just conflict resolution.

Spending time in this space can help us see what matters most. This is an excellent tool for you, your spouse, and your children. Your child might have an exam coming up and need some reflection on their task at hand. Your spouse might have an important meeting coming tomorrow that determines whether they get promoted or not. You might need time to mull over personal goals yourself. You've decided to become a mindful family, and that's a goal on its own. Your son is taking an exam that determines whether he is accepted into a certain university. What is the most important thing in life at that moment? Is the fact that his girlfriend is moving to another state the most important aspect of his life, or is it passing the exam?

Life has become a fast-moving, technologically filled empire that waits for no one. Yes, we remain in the present because it's the only place we survive; however, thinking about desires and passions for our future is what fuels us with motivation. We wouldn't want to miss out on this.

You might be going through a difficult time right now because your mother passed away. You've been walking with this substantially oppressing grief every day since, and it weighs you down. You haven't paid much attention to your family, and those crucial bonds are drifting away from you dangerously. I'm sure your family understands, but you have responsibilities as well. This chair can help us in this situation, too, because we cannot escape life's happenings; we can only see what matters most at the time. Your family needs you, and you can awaken their views in your mind.

Another great aspect of this silent time is for healing purposes. Our emotional distress isn't always tied to anger and fear. Sometimes, we are saddened by the loss of a loved one, a job, or even a car that was stolen. It's fine because you're allowed to grieve a loss. My point is this: Have you ever been to a hospital that didn't resemble a library? The nurses urge you to be quiet and hush you whenever you become a nuisance to the patients. It's obvious why they do this, and I understand it fully. The patients in that hospital require quiet time to heal from their physical and emotional wounds. You can't argue with a practice that is as old as medicine itself.

You don't want your trauma or sadness to spread into your life. You want to deal with it right away. Our bodies go into a recuperative stage when our brain waves slow down. That's why we tend to feel great after a good night's rest. The only difference is that you're introducing your mind to suggested rest when you sit there.

Finally, there is one more advantage of utter silence. I am not going to preach to you, but there is a balance between positive and negative, good and bad, and finally, chaos and peace. We can become connected to ourselves through spirituality. It's something we often overlook in the modern day and age, but our spirit is there, and it needs guidance. Have you seen how long Buddhist monks live? You would think they've drunk from the fountain of youth.

The fact is that they live longer because they lead prosperous and spiritual lives. They accept that there's a higher being and a higher purpose for their existence. This mindful and spiritual connection they maintain is what keeps them going into a ripe old age. I know I want to grow old, I wish my husband to grow old, and I sure want my kids to reach 100. I've become spiritual myself, and once again, I will not lead you to a specific teaching, but I've benefited immensely. I know where my place is, and I know that there's always a power that's greater than me. Feel free to welcome and embrace it.

The Practice of Sitting Quiet for Kids

I've mentioned how hard it was to teach my kids the art of silence in the beginning, and I would never sugar-coat something like that. There's no set way of doing it, but I'll share some tips with you.

I motivated my children with the comfort of the chair itself when I made sure it couldn't feel like anything but heaven. One could honestly sleep in it. Mindfulness, whether it's meditation or relaxation, introduces us to the valuable art of sitting in the most comfortable position we can find. Don't let this deter you from the position I've spoken of when you are deep in meditation, but your kids aren't going to sit like a lotus. Quite frankly, it's not entirely necessary, especially for beginners.

The second tactic of mine was to give them direction in relaxation. I provided headphones, and the first few times, they were allowed to listen to music. Any music was fine except for the fact that it had to be peaceful. No rock and roll or heavy metal was allowed. Honestly, today's children listen to the weirdest things, and I'm not speaking from a Jurassic age. One generation is enough to cross the line with musical taste. I prefer instrumental classics in my quiet time, but my children were allowed to choose. It was a few weeks before I added a playlist with guided meditation and background music.

I only began teaching them the techniques in this book when they wanted me to do so. They saw a change in my spouse and myself and wanted to feel the way we did. That's when I taught them about breathing, the present moment, and using an anchor point in their bodies to focus their emotions on. My kids continued the practice when they noticed the detachment from their thoughts through carefully instructed mindfulness.

There you have it. Now I know you're not comparing my chair of disputes to some fantasy program, and I suggest you get to work on it right away. You can implement this while you work on your own mindfulness and peaceful parenting.

CHAPTER 10:

MINDFULNESS PRACTICES FOR THE WHOLE FAMILY

This book is filled with practices, exercises, and techniques that can enhance every family member's stance in their home and life. This lifestyle can improve a husband's ability to cope with his workload, mashing up with home life. Financial strains are burdensome, and this can cause the family to divide under pressure. It doesn't matter who the breadwinner is and who the homemaker is. So many families see both parents working nowadays, and the children are under someone else's care.

Concerns for children's safety become integrated anxiety in the minds of parents, whether they're at home, at school, or even on a camping trip with friends. Kid's lives become busier by the day, and they can forget to enjoy the scenery along life's journey. Irrespective, I'm going to focus on mindful practices for each and every member individually, as well as give you the meditation session I promised. One final piece of advice is to imagine my voice if you're reading this chapter. Really listen to it and use your unconscious mind to welcome the sounds.

Mindfulness for Moms

There are a few more tips I want to provide you before we go into a session, because I've missed some elements, some of which will correlate to newborn moms. Breathing, body scans, and the present moment remain vital practices. But with newborn babies, we can find ourselves becoming mindless again. Use the three main methods of centering yourself, as well as the few I'll discuss here.

Moms of newborn babies can find themselves seated a lot, and they should use this to their advantage. Focus on grounding yourself to the seat below when you're breastfeeding. Keep your feet flat on the ground, and your weight evenly distributed. Use mindful breathing for the duration of your feeding.

Listen to sounds nearby if you can't focus on your breathing. The dishwasher might be making a whirring noise or the clock ticking on the mantle. Try to identify three sounds that you can focus on simultaneously.

Use muscle tension releases in your body scan and express gratitude when you feel overwhelmed. I sit deep in thought and find a minimum of five things I'm grateful for and then repeat them out loud.

Remember to be kind to yourself and don't allow judgment from your mind. Go back to practicing awareness and observe thoughts from a distance. Don't alter them or interfere in any way. If you struggle to stop the speed at which they're moving, take a walk. You can do this with your baby, and the two of you breathe fresh air while noticing interesting aspects of nature. These are all pragmatic forms of mindfulness for new moms.

Now I'll share a meditation session with you that I've designed for moms alone. It's a guided imagery meditation, and you're welcome to use the chair of disputes to find ultimate comfort through it.

Mom's Session

Sit back, relax, and find comfort in my voice, because I wish to guide you into a submissive yet mindful state. There is nothing to fear while you hear my voice. Begin with your breathing as you press your feet firmly into the ground and your spine evenly against the backrest. Place your arms on the armrests and connect to the texture of it. Feel it with your fingers as it touches your skin. Use headphones to gain the full experience if you're listening to my voice. The tone of sounds is welcoming, and you take a deep breath in through your nose as you hold it there. Your diaphragm is expanding, and the air feels light in your lungs. Press it out through your mouth as your chest moves closer to the seat.

Take another deep breath in and pay attention to your expansion as your skin keeps caressing the material beneath it. Now guide the air back out through your mouth and feel the coolness as it passes through your throat. There is perhaps a gentle tingle under your feet where it touches the earth, and you welcome the sensation before taking another deep, slow breath. Focus on the way your body rises and falls and my voice grows gradually louder with each inhale. I need you to continue breathing this way ten more times, counting each one and paying attention to the sensations in your feet and hands. The tingling in your feet strengthens its attraction with each passing moment. Your hands and arms are melting into the surface they touch. When you reach five deep breaths, the sensation in your feet will progress to another level, one which draws your attention strongly.

It's okay to shift your focus as long as you continue the even flow of your breaths. You feel an urge to connect your feet with the earth and no longer want the sensation that resides in them. Breath seven will pull a deeper, slower breath in, and you follow it as it extends to your stomach. Notice how your mid-section rises. You exhale and concentrate on the diminishment of these feelings in your feet. A thought creeps into your mind, and you know what those feelings in your toes are. Keep breathing and counting as your mind expresses the fear it feels. You worry about your family, and this feeling has manifested itself in your bottom limbs now.

Don't be afraid of the emotion but focus back on your breathing for a moment. Can you feel how even it has become? You can feel your heart beating in your chest, and the rhythm is slightly out of tune. Acknowledge the existence of this fearful figure that's resisting the connection to the earth. It began as a familiar sensation that deceived you into believing it was welcoming. I want you to take another three deep breaths as you intend to calm the arrhythmia in your heart. The organ is labored by the feelings in your feet. Feel the air embrace your lungs and tickle the walls of your veins as it moves out again. The second intake of air is cooler, and it caresses your inner body. Hold this one for a little longer and allow the air to escape into your heart.

Exhale entirely and take the third breath in as you focus on the second visit to your loving organ. The air is cleansing it, and the next beat is gentler. Follow the air out of your body and continue breathing evenly again. Listen to your heartbeat now, and recognize a perfect rhythm in it. You may feel tired now because fear is a thief who steals your energy. It has attacked your heart, and you have managed to correct the beats now. Take a few moments and just keep listening to the gentle pumps from this large muscle in your chest. It is stronger now, and you realize that fear is only a feeling. It's a foreign invader in your body and needs to exit.

Take another deeper, slower breath and shift your attention back to your feet. You accept that this fear of failure has prevented you from grounding yourself. You don't want this anymore, and the alien will be forced out of your energy space. The feeling in your feet starts fading slowly as you keep taking fresh air in through the nose and out through the mouth. Your entire body has relaxed into the surface you sit on, and it is time for your feet to meet the same fate. Feel the strength inside of you as it gains momentum. Those gentle rhythms in your heart encourage it to grow more with each breath. The only thing that overwhelms you now is the comfort of your own strength. Give in to it and feel the sensation dissipate. Your feet are slowly connecting to the earth below you, and all sensations are returning to normal.

Bathe in the ultimate security of your decision and accept that fear is only an emotion. Breathe deeply and count backward now. The first breath begins at five, and your heart increases its rhythm ever so slightly.

Four, and it gains more liveliness. Three, and your body is retaining some weight again. Two, and your mind is awakening to its usual alertness. One, and you are back in your physical presence. Your body has always been here with you where you are right now. Look around the room and move your attention to something you can see. Don't forget the feelings you experienced and the coziness in your soul as you awaken fully.

Mindfulness for Dads

Responsibility to our families is one of the first sensations that hit fathers when their children are born. They want to provide a safe and financially secure environment for their family, as well as give them the life they deserve. Dads become flabbergasted with unwanted thoughts and emotions that can show up unknowingly. A man is not immune to stress. Dads should practice all the techniques in this book to help them overcome distress and improve their lives so that they may be the role model their children need.

Men are generalized as poor listeners, and what people forget is that it's difficult to listen no matter who you are, woman or man. The first advice I can give you is to exercise listening skills with your spouse. Sit across from each other as each person spends three minutes telling a story. The other person must repeat the story back as they heard it. This helps us exercise our hearing abilities.

The second exercise partners can practice is empathy. Do the same three-minute session, except with one alteration. The partner who relays the message back isn't going to use words. They must translate their spouse's story into emotions. How did your spouse feel when they spoke of the trip to the zoo yesterday? Describe every feeling with words.

The final advice for dads is that you remember to take those pauses, because men need them too. Don't act tough and think you're more resilient because that's what is expected of you. You are also human, and you should always stop, drop, and roll thoughts in your mind as you reflect on different responses.

I've compiled a guided imagery meditation for dads too.

Dad's Session

Find your comfort as I guide you into subliminal imagery. Your mind will remain fully aware through the session, and all urges to drift away will drift away themselves. I'm certain that you are tense, as fathers normally are, and I need you to resist the tension in your body. Use the power of your intention to forget about the tightness in your muscles. Place your left hand on your stomach and pull a deep breath as you listen to the air passing through your nostrils. It's a faint sound, but it will grow louder with each inhalation. You can feel your hand rise subtly, and you keep the air in your chest for a moment. Press it out through your lips now and sink slightly into the chair beneath you.

Place your right hand on your chest, if you can, and take another deep breath. Notice how your chest rises well above your stomach region and hear the sounds of breath passing through your nose. Hold it as long as you feel comfortable and press it out slowly again. Don't stop listening to my voice as you continue to take breaths and hold them. The act of holding the air brings your body to a calmer state each time. You are stressed and very rarely feel calm in your life. Deepen the relaxation more with five more deep breaths. Your chest rises close to the heavens each time, and your body melts into a further comfort.

You can feel the fabric of the couch beneath you, and your body is becoming heavier. The urge to become one with the seat is unbearable. Your breathing is becoming more natural, and you can move your arms back down now. Grow the desire to relax more with each word I speak and every breath you take. The air is soothing on your tongue as it passes through your mouth. You can hear it clearly now. Tickle your tongue with this amazing feeling five more times and sink deeper into the chair. Your body has fallen into a state of relaxation that you've forgotten about. The last time you felt this good was when you were a young kid. Can you remember that in the present moment?

92

You can see the memory, but you can't touch it because you're drifting through the storage in your mind. It hasn't been tangible for years now, but it brings a smile across your face. Keep breathing as you mentally swipe right on the images in front of you, moving further ahead in your life. You can move the images as you can conform time in the present. However, they're merely fragments of a time that once was. You are in full control. Keep browsing as you pass through your school years and slow down to the moment you saw yourself in your current career. Career day at school was a memorable event, and you acknowledge how far you've come since. You accept the hard work you've put into getting here.

You flick your finger to move the "timed images" again, and the next one that grabs your attention is the day you met your gorgeous wife. Your body is experiencing the emotions you felt that day. They are causing sensations in various places right now. Connect the memory to the present feelings in your system. Continue breathing evenly as you flick your finger once more. There's an image from memory that alters your present sensations slightly now. It was in the doctor's office when your wife was having an ultrasound. Watch your face as you light up with excitement and curiosity. Your body keeps reminding you of the feelings you experienced back then. You can see the thoughts that crossed your mind while you stood over your wife. Your face resembles someone who can't wait for the future, someone who didn't know how to live in the present yet.

Never mind the memory too much because it can't change anything in the present time. You can only recognize it for an image in your mind, one that makes you happy. You welcome the most important thought into your present space from that memory. It was an acknowledgment that hit you as the screen lit up with an image of your child. You can remember how you imagined they would be. You saw yourself as a provider of security and love, compassion and fearlessness. You knew at that moment that you had the power to choose the destiny of that child.

Your hand touches your wife's in the memory recollection, and you can feel the same intimacy in your present hand. The sensation reminds you that your wife has faith in your abilities to offer them a life people dream of. There is nothing that can overpower the knowledge and acceptance in your mind as you used your ability to shape time in the present, to see what mattered in the past. There was a reality that you've forgotten now, and you needed to be reminded of it. You're welcome to embrace memories further down the line, but once you're done, come back to your spatial body. Feel the fabric against your skin again as you focus on your breathing again. Listen to the air passing through your nostrils and into your lungs. Your body is separating from the surface now, and you are disconnected from past influences. The only time that matters is the present, and I want you to return to it fully. You've never left but allowed your past to surface so that you can be aware of the feelings you experience in the present.

Breathe deeply and press the air out. Count to two as you listen for sounds other than my voice and the air in your lungs. Count to three when you feel your bottom scratching the fabric. Count to four as you take another breath and move your hand to feel your chest. Count to five on the final breath as you are fully alert again. Take a moment to recognize the change in your present feelings. You know that you won't fail your family because the seed to do right was planted many years ago.

Mindfulness for Kids

How could I forget teens and children? Not a chance! This is a family team effort, after all. I'm sure your parents have been teaching you mindful techniques as they learn them, and it's a pleasure introducing you to the chair of disputes. I know that you're enjoying that. However, mindless behavior doesn't discriminate, and it will impact your lives too. The moment you learn about the brain and its mindful presence is the moment you start enjoying life. I can get technical if you wish, but I won't bore you with too much of it. I'll only briefly explain what happens to pique your interest because I know you love learning.

The brainstem is the bottom part of your brain, and it's responsible for physical interactions in your body, such as breathing. The limbic system sits higher up and activates our emotions and memory. The prefrontal cortex is the front portion of our brains and is the bugger that controls our thoughts. Mindfulness is targeted at the prefrontal cortex and limbic systems because they are the reason we feel down or stressed out before an exam. Mindless humans have miniature-sized monkeys in their brains who jump erratically from branch to branch in each of the segments in our brains. We use techniques to cage these disruptive creatures and take back control (Beach, 2014).

Anyway, your parents have been sharing new methods with you, which include silent time. This is in no way a punishment because I've convinced them not to do that anymore. It's counterproductive and harmful, as you know. There is one more piece of news I'd like to share with you before I jump into a session I designed just for you. Kids love technology and apps on their mobile devices, right? Guess what? Mindfulness apps are all over, and I'll name a few that you can download.

Insight Meditation Timer is great for timing your sessions, whereas, *Stop, Breathe, and Think* allows you to customize your guided session with keywords derived from your emotions. *Smiling Mind* is specifically designed for teenagers and comes with a cool British or Australian accent. The last app I can name is called *Take a Break*, and this one is great for reducing stress fast. Go ahead and download your mindful-promoting technology.

Let's get into the session now, and you can also use the chair of disputes for this guided imagery practice.

A Children and Teenage Session

Welcome to my guide. Please allow my voice to carry you into a calmer place. I know your mind is wandering all over the place, but you can do this. In fact, you're capable of anything. Find a comfortable position and listen to my every word. Remember the breathing techniques and focus on the intake of air as you embrace changes. The air flows into your nose and out of your mouth. Drop your eyes somewhat and look at your nose. Children have an amazing capacity for imagination, and I'm going to guide yours now if you'll allow me. Feel the air passing into your lungs as you imagine a color. It can be any color that you like. Blue, green, purple, or pink works just fine. Attach the color mentally to the air that passes into your nose. Don't stop breathing evenly and follow the color in through the nostrils and out through the mouth.

You have given your breathing a physical form and color now. It is hard to notice anything other than the air going in and out. It's a mono-colored flow that enters your body, and every time you press it out of your mouth, it just goes back into your nose. The color deepens with every word you hear, and you can feel a gentle relaxation knocking on your door, waiting to reach further into your body. The color is providing the entrance alongside the sounds you hear. Take a deeper breath now and open your system to comfort as it enters with the color. You begin feeling weightless and wish to feel even calmer. Take another deep breath, and welcome more calm into your body space. The color has grown even deeper as you feel your body in a floating state. You want to go even deeper as you breathe hard once more. The moment you let go of the breath, your mind slips away from the color, and you are shifted to a new image.

You can see a virtual jungle in front of you that's filled with various shades of green, brown, beige, and attractive colors from all the pretty flowers. Your mental image has changed because you reached the ultimate relaxation you desired. Don't stop breathing because you don't want any tension to enter this magnetizing image you've created. There's a certain peace in this space where you are right now, and you can feel it with your body. The connection to physical sensations never wavers because you are stuck in the present moment. Suddenly, something catches your inner eye, and you shift your focus to the movement. This is followed by another swift movement, and you catch a glimpse of a bright yellow object.

I want you to focus harder on the trees now and notice what you see on the branches. Monkeys. There are monkeys everywhere! You are surrounded by apes throwing bananas at each other from the various branches. A new sound begins to enter your present space, and it's very noisy. The monkeys are screeching at each other in their warzone. Bananas are flying aimlessly, and the monkeys look aggressive. They are jumping up and down on the branches and flinging more bananas in the air. I know this image is rather entertaining, but I want you to focus on my voice now. It remains louder than the monkey's war cries.

Think about every skill your parents have given you to create peace in a war-torn jungle. The breathing exercises and the present time manipulation. You find yourself counting from ten to one slowly as you think of each lesson you've learned. The monkeys attempt to distract you as a banana hits your head. Don't give them a second chance! Take a deep breath in and hold it as the image in front of you slows down. Release the air and focus on one monkey at a time. Look at it as you draw another deep breath and watch it freeze when you exhale. Take a moment to feel the emotions that resemble bananas right now. You are overwhelmed and afraid of this battle of the apes in front of you; however, it only lasts a second, and you take another deep breath. Look as another monkey pauses in his actions and release the air from your lungs gently. He was the ape that was throwing fear around.

Take another breath and slow down the monkey throwing disappointment bananas at his teammates. There's a sense of achievement as you stop him in his tracks. Keep doing this until you come to the last monkey. This one has been a constant battle in your jungle, always instigating fights between the other branches of monkeys. Look him in the eyes and feel the power of the breath you draw. His face is concerned, and he flings one more doubtful banana your way before you press the air out gently. The banana of self-doubt falls to the ground in front of your virtual feet, and you have a deep calmness that reaches your soul.

It touches your heart as you take another breath and feel the jungle fade slowly. The second deep breath moves the previous battlefield into a blurry state. The third breath sends the image into mental storage, and the fourth inhale brings your subconscious mind back to the chair you never left. The fifth breath you pull into your lungs is the one that makes you realize that you are capable of great things and living a peaceful life. Watch the faded color exit your mouth as you press the air out of your lungs.

You have given yourself to a journey into the jungle of your mind, and I'm proud of you for ending the war. Your mind is at peace now, and so is your relationship with your parents and siblings. You can finally understand how valuable the guidance is that they're teaching you as you sit in your comfortable position, feeling relaxed in your entire body. Well done. You've completed your first imagery meditation.

CONCLUSION

Parenting is a glorious time of our lives, but it also poses many challenges daily. The first few years are particularly trying for us. This doesn't mean we love our children and families any less, though. We all live different lives, and your age, career, gender, and spiritual aspirations don't change a thing. Let's face it, parenting is a career of its own. So many people want to give us the skills to achieve thoughtful parenting, but their advice often lacks sustenance. The world is flooded with many good reads, and I won't deny that, but so many books miss one or two key elements. I am a parent, and I know my only goal in life is to see my child succeed happily in theirs. I've spent years finding information that worked for me and countless others.

I've shoved the superficial information aside and focused on using the methods proven to reach the root of any problem in our lives. I've come to know that children are also human beings, and they're just as fragile as we are. They too suffer from stress and fear. They succumb to anger, humiliation, and retaliation. This stirs unrest in our peaceful lives. Kids have learned to bury their pain so deep that we can't see it, and it bursts at the most inappropriate times. Chaos and unease enter our families because we are a single unit, no matter how much some may try to deviate. The mind is the most powerful tool any human possesses, and when it goes along the beaten track, we become mindless beings who can't cope with life.

We need to place our minds under a microscope and identify the initial triggers for an upset. How do these things alter the peaceful silence that should be natural? Instead, there's a flurry of disturbance in our quiet, and it can reach a stage where we feel surrender is the only option. This is a recipe for disaster, and the consequences alone can interfere with our ability to live life to the fullest. Mindfulness and peaceful parenting allow us to break free from the prison of noise and understand the silence we need to conduct our decisions. They introduce this priceless commodity into our existence again because it's something that never left. Humans have the ability to compose their own sheet music and don't need to be influenced by these traits.

Peaceful parenting and mindful teachings work hand-in-hand to bring us back to the only place that matters, here. There's no other time that's more relevant to change things in our favor. We take back control when we become aware of our present surroundings and the actions of our bodies. It doesn't matter what you're doing; the fact is that you're living life right now. Yes, even if you're driving to your son's football game and got stuck in traffic along the way. Who wants life to pass them by without being there? It's all part of the human experience, and we can enjoy it every moment. There's nothing stopping us from raising independent and mindful children and becoming our best possible selves. Practical techniques will bring your mind to this desired state before you know it.

Parents frequently live with anxiety and fear the unknown future. They even question their abilities as parents. These so-called premonitions in our minds distract us from being parents every day. The worst of all is that your children suffer from this anxiety too. It permeates through the family and takes no prisoners. Mindfulness is an evidence-based technique, as I've shown you throughout the book. Psychology and science agree that it's an effective method to overcome stress, worries, depression, and even physical sickness. Studies have shown how our influence on children's behavior today will continue until they're old and gray. No one can ever wish constant anxiety upon their own blood.

I've shared the knowledge I gained with you so that the constant conflict in your home and life can finally come to an end. Stop worrying about your children, because you can help them develop the tools they need to avoid dangers in the modern world. It doesn't matter how busy life gets; we can always come back to our mindful state to breach it. Continue practicing peaceful parenting to ensure that war is no longer a threat and that stress can't harm anyone in your family. This is when you work together and defeat obstacles that stand in your way.

I've given you skills and knowledge that include:

- An in-depth perception of mindfulness and meditation
- Introductions to the peaceful parenting way of life and how to implement it
- Removing daily stressors and problems through mindful meditation
- Living a universal and adaptable life in peace through remarkable parenting
- Knowing how to love life again by enjoying parenthood and family life
- Various meditation sessions that differ in duration and power
- Manipulating time in any event and circumstance
- Using tactics that reveal what matters most and the actions needed to arrive there
- Creating a mindful home where the best mother, father, child, husband, and wife live harmoniously

You can tick one thing off your list of concerns because I've given you the method to overcome chaos in the family, and I've used language that children can understand as well. The examples in this book will provide you with answers to so many questions because they're easily relatable. Remove the complexity of mindless living from your life today with the easy exercises you've learned about. Don't beat yourself up, because we can all be duped by the appearance of mindless thoughts. We simply need to stop them before they gather momentum and harm our mental and physical wellbeing.

You are no longer deceived by thoughtlessness, and it has no power over you anymore. You can hear the calmness of joyful life experience calling your name. Answer it while you're listening intently. Mindfulness and peaceful parenting will lead you to productivity, success, happiness, and a fruitful family life. Go ahead and be who you deserve to be.

The only thing left to say is that you believe in yourself. Never allow doubt to creep in, because anyone can do this. People have been at it for thousands of years.

I'D LOVE YOUR HELP

As a self-publishing author, reviews are the lifeblood of my work.

I would be over-the-moon thankful if you could take just 60 seconds to leave a brief review on Amazon.

I know you must be busy and I truly appreciate your time, even a few short sentences would be greatly helpful.

Don't forget to get your complimentary

MINDFULNESS SIGNS:

STAY IN THE MOMENT

Mindful enough? I hope you are!

With this download, you'll get 5 free printable signs that:

- Will immediately get you back to the present moment;
- Are specifically designed to bring awareness and mindfulness;
- Are easy to hang on a wall, stick on the fridge or anywhere else;
- Hang them everywhere, notice them, and come back to the now!

Mindfulness is a powerful tool for productivity, focus and calmness.

Go ahead and click on the link below to get your free mindful signs:

http://gracestockholm.net/peaceful-parenting-and-mindfulness-fridge-signs/

BONUS SECTION:
GUIDED MEDITATION FOR PARENTS AND KIDS

In this bonus section, I have prepared 2 special full guided meditation sessions.

The first is for you, the parent. As we have learned throughout the book, meditating is a great way to relieve stress and keep composure throughout our hectic lives. It is crucial to practice meditation if you want to live a mindful life. In this meditation, we will focus on the breath, our inner peace and keeping mindful.

The second session is for your child. In this session your child will learn the benefits of meditating as well as be more empowered and focused. Here to we will focus on breathing, peace and mindfulness. This practice is suitable for children of all ages. Depending on your child's age, you may want to sit with your child for this session, at least for the first few times. If you have a younger child and the session is too long for them, simply do a few minutes at a time and gradually increase the meditation time.

If this is the audio version, just dive in.

If this is the kindle or paperback version, sit down and read it to yourself slowly.

Session #1 - For You

-Welcome to this meditation practice for mindfulness. During the practice today, we're going to be exploring the mind, the body, the thoughts and emotions that make us who we are. Mindfulness is the easiest way to thrive in life, regardless of what you're about to do.

-The best practical way to experience mindfulness is to meditate. Meditation is nothing but sitting down, creating a comfortable posture for yourself, and then focusing on your breathing while observing your thoughts and feelings. Most of the time, meditations will be guided, like this one, so that you can have a better overall experience.

-For the most part today, we will be focusing on the breath, the absolute pillar between your conscious and unconscious thinking. Focusing on the simple act of breathing and making a habit out of it will elevate your wellbeing to unprecedented status.

-Before doing anything else, what I need you to do is to find your posture. The posture is extremely important while meditating. It has to be a relaxed posture, a state in which the body is not tensed, but alert. You need to make sure you're aware of the points of contact between the body and wherever it is that you've decided to stay.

-You can either sit on the floor in a lotus position, arms resting on your knees, spine erect. You can also sit on a chair, hands in your lap, feet touching the floor. Or, you can simply sit on the bed, laying flat and comfortable, hands resting comfortably on your sides. The best posture is the one that makes you feel comfortable and that you can hold onto for an hour without it becoming stressful for the body.

-Now that you've got your posture ready, we will begin the meditation practice by experimenting with the breath. Slowly become more and more aware of your breathing as the body gets comfortable with the posture. Connect your mind with the body, which is possible by connecting the breathing with the thinking. As you notice a thought passing through the mind, immediately turn your attention to the rising and falling of the breath.

-For a few moments now, what I want you to do is to exercise full attention to the breath. You will do this by taking exactly seven full, deep breaths. I will count them with you. With these breaths, the main idea is to be focused entirely on the sounds, the movements, and the feelings these breaths will create throughout your mind and body.

-Make these breaths long, relaxed, loud and clear. Cleanse the body of any tension, emotion, stress, or whatever else you might find unnecessary. Here we go.

-Breathe in through the nose gently, but powerfully, sensing the air flowing down to the lungs. Release the air and breathe gently out through the mouth.

-Again, breathe in through the nose, feeling the way the chest expands, and then breathe out through the mouth, feeling the pressure of the air exiting through the mouth.

-One more time, take a full, deep breath in through the nose, feeling the chest expanding as you do so. And now exhale through the mouth gently, but powerfully, to become even more aware of the breathing process.

-Repeat these breaths for just four more times now. Relaxing more and more as you do so. Becoming more and more aware of the breathing, what it represents, and why it's so essential for us. Completely letting go of any thoughts, feelings, and emotions, you might have started this meditation practice with. They're gone now. There's nothing left but you and the breath.

-And with the last exhale, slowly close your eyes and let the breath come back to its natural state, flowing gently in and out through the nose.

-We will continue to focus on the breath all the way through this entire session. Whenever we feel lost, the first thing we will do is to come back to the breath. That's going to be our safety net, today with the practice, but also throughout the rest of your activities later on.

-Just as we did with the breaths now, we will start a complete scan of our body in a few moments. During the scan, we will be focusing not just on the different parts of the body, but also on releasing any tensions or pain spots we might encounter along the way. Using the power of the breath, we will let everything go without judgment.

-Let's start this body scan from the very tip of your toes today. Notice how the feet are feeling right now. Is there any tension or stress in there? Are the feet hurting, maybe from walking all day today? Are they numb from you not moving them for a few minutes now? With the next following breath, all of the stress, tension, and pain in the feet will go away.

-We will focus on the knees and the rest of the legs now. The knees are some of the most solicited parts of the moving human body. It takes the weight of the body and moves it around like the most magical machine ever created. Observe the knee, the muscles, the entire legs at once. Any tension, any pain, any discomfort will be left to go with this next breath in and out through the nose.

-You are doing great now. Let's move along and up the body. Reaching the stomach and lower back areas of your machinery. Simply notice any discomfort that might be going on right now in these two parts of the body. Do you feel any tension? Pain? Where are these points of stress located more precisely? Remember that your only job is to notice these stress points and do absolutely nothing about them. You don't have to because, with this next breath, all of the tensions will be left to disappear.

-Moving on, we have now reached the upper part of the body, mainly the chest and the upper back. As with the knees, the upper back is also a significant part of the moving body, the body that makes us go from place to place. Also, the chest area is home to the heart, the pumping motor of the entire system.

-Try to feel, just for a moment now, the power of the heart. Imagine you're seeing your heart working effortlessly inside your chest. Wonder at its immaculate creation and incredible ingenuity. And as you do so, scan the chest and the upper back for any tension. And release the tension or stress that you find with the next breath.

-Reaching the last part of the body we're going to be scanning today, just take a moment to enjoy the simplicity of the head and the neck supporting it. The one place where everything happens, the brain, is safely enclosed in a space that's hard and protected, yet feels so natural and mundane. Notice if there's any tension in the neck or head. If you find something that's troubling, do absolutely nothing about it as you will simply breathe and let it go.

-Breathe in through the nose and then out through the nose. Let go of any stress, any pain, any tension, or any uncomfortable thought, feeling or emotion you might be experiencing right now. Let go of anything that is unwanted, but you somehow hold close to you for no reason. Let go of the mindless chatter and remember to come back to the breath whenever the mind goes a little too far into the thinking world, the world of the imagined, the past or the future.

-Awesome job! You are doing great.

-Breathing in and out through the nose now, we will be focusing on a few powerful statements or affirmations about the breath. The most important and unique feature of the body. Breathing, so simple, yet so life-altering.

-Here we go, simply focus on the breathing while the mind takes care of storing these few following affirmations deep within.

-The breath is all that I've got. Between one inhale and one exhale happens the entirety of my life.

The breath is all that I've got. Between one inhale and one exhale happens the entirety of my life.

<<PAUSE FOR 5 SECONDS>>

-Perfect. Everything starts and ends with a breath. It's our most valuable asset, yet something that we rarely pay too much attention to. We're now going to listen to the second affirmation, keeping a gentle focus on the breath.

-Breathing is the first and last act of life. Mastering the art of breathing correctly will ensure a blissful life between the first and last breaths.

Breathing is the first and last act of life. Mastering the art of breathing correctly will ensure a blissful life between the first and

last breaths.

<<PAUSE FOR 5 SECONDS>>

-Very good! When you know how to breathe, you know how to live. Being blissful in life means you've figured out the importance of being alive and of each and every breath. Here we go for the third affirmation. I know it's there, but remember to breathe in and out through the nose.

-Breaths are the links between the mind and the body. Whenever the connection is lost, all I have to do is to start breathing again consciously.

Breaths are the links between the mind and the body. Whenever the connection is lost, all I have to do is to start breathing again consciously.

<<PAUSE FOR 5 SECONDS>>

-You are incorporating these affirmations into your being with ease. Breathing gets us back on track while using the mind as well as the body. It's the one thing that links the material and the spiritual. Gently breathe in and out through the nose while listening to this next one quote.

-Breathe it all in. Love it all out. As long as I'm breathing, it's never too late to start on a new beginning.

Breathe it all in. Love it all out. As long as I'm breathing, it's never too late to start on a new beginning.

<<PAUSE FOR 5 SECONDS>>

-Perfect. The only thing that's constant in life is breathing. Everything else can and will be subject to change, to adversity. We have one more to go before a little break, and then we'll be one step closer to the ending part of the affirmations practice today.

-Thoughts, feelings, and emotions come and go like clouds in a windy sky. Conscious breathing is my anchor.

Thoughts, feelings, and emotions come and go like clouds in a windy sky. Conscious breathing is my anchor.

<<PAUSE FOR 5 SECONDS>>

-Wonderfully done. Take a moment to sit quietly and appreciate the way the mind and the body feel right now. Enjoy this state of complete calm, bliss, and easiness. There's nothing left to do, just enjoy the moment, the present, the now, the only thing you can count on.

-Good job, we'll now resume our affirmations practice. Once again, we will be focusing on these affirmations as well as the breath, combining the two for the ultimate experience. Here we go.

-Breathe. Let go. Remind yourself that this very moment is the only one you know you have for sure.

Breathe. Let go. Remind yourself that this very moment is the only one you know you have for sure.

<<PAUSE FOR 5 SECONDS>>

-Very well. You are doing great getting all of this vital information deep within your system. These affirmations will prove helpful when you least expect it. Here we go with the next one.

-Inhale the future, exhale the past. The trick to life is just to keep breathing. Learn how to exhale, the inhale will take care of itself.

Inhale the future, exhale the past. The trick to life is just to keep breathing. Learn how to exhale, the inhale will take care of itself.

<<PAUSE FOR 5 SECONDS>>

-Good. Both inhalations and exhalations are vital for us humans and all creatures on this planet. Remember to breathe whatever you may encounter. Here we go for the next affirmation for the day. Here it comes, so focus on it.

-When the breath is unsteady, all is unsteady; when the breath is still, all is still. Control your breathing carefully. Inhalation gives strength and a controlled body; retention gives steadiness of

111

mind and longevity; exhalation purifies body and spirit.

When the breath is unsteady, all is unsteady; when the breath is still, all is still. Control your breathing carefully. Inhalation gives strength and a controlled body; retention gives steadiness of mind and longevity; exhalation purifies body and spirit.

<<PAUSE FOR 5 SECONDS>>

-Perfectly done. Keeping a steady breath that's controlled and not happening at random will ensure a more stable overall mind and body process. Let's listen to this last affirmation now.

-What is the wisest one-word sentence that any god, guru, knowledgeable person can say? What is the one word that defines life, being human and alive? What is the word of life? Breathe.

What is the wisest one-word sentence that any god, guru, knowledgeable person can say? What is the one word that defines life, being human and alive? What is the word of life? Breathe.

<<PAUSE FOR 5 SECONDS>>

-Nice one! Breathing is the ultimate proof of life and its existence. As long as you're breathing, you're not missing anything. Breathe, live life, and stay aware of it. It means everything.

-And just for a few moments now, what I need you to do is to simply let the mind do whatever it wants. If the mind goes on thinking, let it think about whatever it wants. If the mind stays quiet, let it be quiet. Whatever the mind decides on doing for the next few seconds now, simply let it do whatever it wants without any judgment. Let go of any focus on the thoughts, feelings, emotions, and even on the breath for now.

<<PAUSE FOR 10 SECONDS>>

-And now gently bring the attention back to the breath. Slowly focusing on the breaths going in through the nose, and then out through the nose again.

112

-Awesome! Let's now move on to the next part of our practice, which is a visualization technique designed to keep you light and peaceful during the meditation, as well as whenever you need to become aware of the power of your mind.

-The practice is very powerful and productive, so pay close attention to the exact technique for the ultimate understanding and experience.

-For a moment now, I want you to visualize a beam of light simply coming down from above your head and onto your body. This beam of light is white and has no scent or particular appearance rather than a simple, calm cascade of delicate rays of light.

-As you notice the beam of light cascading down from above you, and becoming more and more aware of it, you start to notice a few changes all over the body. The breath is becoming more and more relaxed. You have to put in no effort at all for this to happen. It is just that. Once the beam of light is over the top of your head, this slowing of the breath just happens on its own.

-Also, the muscles in the body become less and less tense. There's no tension, no aching, no soreness in the muscles of your body. They simply relax more and more and become still, calm, without having the natural urge to clench up with every distressing thought or unwanted emotion.

-The beam of light is now flowing right through your body, starting to fill the body up with the healing light. This light will slowly rise up all the way to the top of the head, and once that's done, it will leave the body completely still, relaxed and peaceful. Once the body and the mind have been filled with the light, there's nothing that will get you back into the state of stress or unease as long as you'll remember the light pouring down all through the body.

-Begin by noticing the first part of the toes and feet starting to fill up with the light. As the beam moves through the body and hits the toes and the feet, they become soft, light, easy. There's no tension in the feet, no pain in the toes, no stress in the bottom of the legs, the ones that are walking you around every day.

-Take a moment to appreciate your feet, this incredibly important part of your body that is put to the test every single day. Be grateful for your feet, your toes, and for every single bone in them.

-The beam of light continues to fill up the legs now, starting with the lower part, going through the knees, and the upper part of them. As the legs become filled with this gentle beam of light passing through them, they become free of pain, free of sorrow, free of tension and unease. They turn into still, relaxed matter which you can feel and enjoy.

-Only pause for one moment now, appreciating the legs, the knees, and the bones in them for what they are able to do for you every minute of every day. Taking you through life, allowing you to walk to wherever you need to go. Be grateful for your legs now.

-Moving on, the beam of light is now filling the lower part of your abdomen, as well as your lower back, with its natural, still qualities. As this part of the body is getting filled up with the light, you notice it becomes relaxed, untensed, without pain. It feels like your stomach is perfectly still, with no bloating, no feeling of tension, nothing. The same happens with the lower back, which is free from tension and pain, relaxed and feeling just like after a rejuvenating massage.

-Take a few moments now to appreciate the stomach and the lower back. Be grateful for the stomach keeping you fed and alive and the lower back allowing you to move day after day without fail.

-As we're now at the middle of our body, take a small break and compare the two parts of it, the lower one which is now filled with the light, and the upper part which is yet to have been filled, and see if you can spot the differences. Is there more calm in one part, more relaxation in one part? Can you appreciate the lower part being more relaxed and less tense than the upper one?

-Gently become more aware of your breathing, which happens effortlessly now, going in through the nose, and then out through the mouth.

-Nice, let's now move along and see the beam of light reaching the upper part of your chest area, the place where some of your most vital organs are placed. Feel the way the beam of light is making your heart, lungs, liver, and other vital organs feel as it touches this part of your body.

-Also, notice how the light makes the upper part of your back become tenseless, painless, stress-free. There's no more struggle for your spine and back to stay fully erect.

-There's no effort on your lungs to breathe, on your heart to beat properly and on your other organs to do their job peacefully.

-Just for a moment now, take in just how grateful you are for your heart beating properly, your lungs breathing the right way, your liver doing its job perfectly. Appreciate the way these organs all work for your wellbeing, and just how lucky you are for having them all healthy and functioning.

-The beam of light has now reached the neck area of the body, filling up almost the entire thing with warmth, calmness and ease. As the light fills up the neck, you can start feeling a relaxed mood of the neck, the part of your body that is supporting the head and the mind, where all of this wonder we call "life" is happening." Once the light fills up the neck, there's no more tension, no more pain, and no more stress in this part of the body.

-Take a second or two to appreciate the neck, this small, yet vital part of the body that you rely on every day. Be grateful for it and enjoy it now, completely free of tension thanks to the light.

-The beam of light is now flowing all through your body now, as it has filled your body all the way up to your head. Feel the light gently enveloping the inside of your face, back of the head and skull. As it does so, notice how every single tension or unease in this part of the body becomes nothing. There's no tension or pain left as the light touches the stress point.

-Really take the time to enjoy this feeling of the head and brain becoming fully still, relaxed and light. Appreciate that you have a working brain and mind, which have now been completely cleansed thanks to this beam of light passing down through the body. Be grateful for them all.

-Wonderful. You've now reached the end of the visualization. But before we part, I want you to forever keep in mind this feeling of ease, calm, and lightness in the body. Starting with the legs, coming up to the abdomen and stomach, lower back, hands, chest, heart, and lungs, reaching the neck and all the way up to the head, the brain, and top of the head.

-Everything is now stress-free, without tension or pain. Remember this feeling and keep it close to you all the way throughout the day.

-And whenever things are becoming uneasy again, and they will, this is part of life, simply visualize the beam of light coming down over your head.

-Whenever things become tense again, close your eyes for a minute, take a few deep breaths in and out, and then let the beam of light show up. Cleansing the body of all the pain and tension points that will arise once in a while. Stay gentle and let the light do what it's supposed to do.

-As we're moving closer to the final steps of this mindful meditation practice today, all you have to do is to regroup and peacefully come back into the body now.

-Begin by noticing the weight of the body on the chair or the floor beneath you. Focus on those points of contact between you and the surface beneath you. Also, feel any contact points your arms are creating, either with the legs or the clothes you're wearing right now.

-Moving on, what I need you to do is to focus on any sounds you might be hearing right now. Activate your sense of sound and try and listen for any sounds that are close, like the ones coming from your room or the room near you, but also those sounds that come from afar, like a car or a dog outside in the street.

-If there are any, you can also focus on any scents or tastes right now. See if there's any smell you can feel through the nose. Also, see if there's anything you can taste in your mouth. If there is one, identify it and let it be, without analyzing it or doing anything else.

-Following the pattern, you will now gently, softly open the eyes, engaging the sense of sight into the full awakening of the mind and body from this meditative state. All you have to do is to come back entirely from it and into the physical world.

-Take a moment to appreciate the sense of ease that you're feeling right now. And remember to use peaceful breathing all throughout the day today to ensure a smooth transition between the mind and the body with every single step that you're taking.

-Becoming mindful is always a game. The mind is so very well trained to have us think of a million things every single moment of our existence. The only way to tame the mind is to remember to become aware of the breathing. Simply doing this will stop the unstoppable chatter that is constantly happening in the mind.

-Once you've broken the link between thoughts, the mind will naturally become quiet and peaceful. There's no way you can stop the mind from thinking. It's like wanting to stop the lungs from breathing, or the legs from carrying you around. Your mind chattering is not the problem. You being too into what the mind is chatting about is the issue.

-Instead, focus on the breath, become present and mindful for as many times and as long as possible every single moment. You'll see it will become natural after a while, but you have to put in the conscious effort at first. As with anything, practice will make it easier and more comfortable.

-Thank you for being part of this meditation practice today. You can listen to the session again whenever you feel like it. It helps if you can listen to it once or twice every week for at least a month, in order for the affirmations and the visualization technique to really stick with you. Enjoy and stay peaceful!

Session #2 - For Your Child

-Hi, and welcome to this meditation practice. Today, we will be focusing on meditation, peace, and mindfulness. If you've read the book for this practice, or if mom or dad told you a bit about what they have learned in the book, then you're one step closer to fully understanding what I'm about to tell you. If you didn't, it's okay. I'm going to explain everything that you should know about these terms as we go along. You don't need to have any previous knowledge about the meditation practice, mindfulness, or peace for you to enjoy this.

-We're going to start this one with a series of questions, which is not something that's usually done when you're meditating. Are you peaceful today? Are you at peace with how the day today has come to be thus far? I'm starting this practice today with some questions because questions are important. Questions help us evolve.

-Do you know what's also important, like questions? Answers. Truthful, honest answers that you give to these questions. Elaborate ones, not just the yes or no type. For example, when someone asks you if you are peaceful today, really try and respond honestly and in detail. Yes, I am peaceful today because of this and that. Or no, I am not peaceful today because of this and that reason.

-Being honest with your own self is the most important thing you can do at all times. Even if you try to, you will never be able to lie to yourself for long. Maybe you will get by once or twice but, eventually, you will know deep within yourself that something doesn't feel right.

-So before we dive deep into the practice today, a practice about peacefulness and calm, about being mindful and still, let's answer this question. Let's establish the true level of peacefulness we're experiencing now, at the start of this meditation.

-Are you peaceful right now? How peaceful compared to yesterday? How peaceful compared to a month ago? How peaceful are you compared to the last time you've gotten into a quarrel at kindergarten or school? How peaceful are you now if you were to compare it to the last time you've got a bad grade? Are you now more peaceful than the last time you've been confused by something?

-I'll let you be for a little while now, as you try and understand your level of peacefulness at this very moment. Just think about it. You don't have to speak or do anything, to write or even move. Just think about it and evaluate the level of peace that you're experiencing right now. Make a mental note of it, and then we'll move along.

<<PAUSE FOR 10 SECONDS>>

-Good job. Now that you know how peaceful or not-so-peaceful you are right now, we can move along. Today, we will be focusing on the very idea of meditation and mindfulness, the basic practice of the ideology. Mindfulness is a way of living, and meditation is the most important practice you can do to be mindful.

-Being mindful means you are aware of every action that you are a part of or initiate. Mindfulness doesn't mean your mind is full and you can't deal with it. On the contrary, mindfulness means that, no matter how busy the mind is, you can cope with it in a peaceful, pleasant way. Instead of reacting to thoughts and emotions, you respond to them in a calm way. This will make so much more sense in a few moments, so bear with me now.

-Before going into the practice today, I will let you in on a few secrets of mindfulness, as well as inform you of the two ways in which you can participate in the meditation today. Regardless of which one of the two methods you'll choose for the practice, you'll still feel the benefits once we're ready with listening to this recording and you following along. This is the great thing about mindfulness and meditation: there's no right or wrong way of doing it!

-Okay, so here it is. Mindfulness is the idea of being present for as long as you can. The best life you can live is the life of the present moment. Dwelling on past events or wondering what the future will bring, can cause us anxiety, uncertainty, and stress. Being present in the moment is the best way to tackle whatever you have to do in life.

-You become present in the now by keeping a constant look on your breathing, as well as your surroundings and your own body. The breath is the most important physical process of the body. Between every inhale and every exhale lies the entirety of your life.

-When you breathe, you exercise the most basic human function, as well as the most divine, spiritual, and intense of all human experiences.

-Breathing is the fundamental process in any meditation, the practice of mindfulness. Daily meditation is the best way to practice mindfulness and exercise the powers of being in the present moment. Simply sitting down and following your breath for even a few minutes every day has incredible health benefits for the mind and body.

-Today, we will be focusing on the idea of breathing and how we can follow the breath while staying in the present moment for longer and longer periods of time. While we will be focusing on the breath, there are two ways in which you can go about your practice today.

-First, you can simply listen to this practice and follow it while doing anything that you do. You can be playing around the house, do some chores, do homework, or anything else that you won't be so distracted by listening to this recording.

-Second, you can fully dedicate yourself to the practice and engage with every single exercise that you'll be hearing for the next hour. You will want to sit down, relax, and follow the breath just like I'll guide you. Whatever you choose to do, remember to carefully listen to the practice for the best outcome.

-For the next few moments now, what I need you to do is sit back, relax, and start noticing the breath. See where in the body the breath is happening. Notice the movement of the breath as it expands and contracts the body. While doing so, try to settle into a comfortable posture. If you're moving around, simply focus on the breathing.

-Now you are ready to take a few big, deep breaths. You'll go in through the nose, slowly filling up your lungs with air, and then out

121

through the mouth, gently releasing the breath. While you take a few more of these powerful breaths, focus on the chest expanding and contracting, on the power of the breathing itself, which can be both intense, and also relaxed, calm, easy.

-Take a few more of these big breaths and focus on the breathing without paying any attention to anything else. Don't worry about thoughts, feelings, emotions, the body, the surroundings you're in, don't worry about anything. Focus just on breathing.

-And now, with your next breath out, close the eyes and let the breath relax back to its natural rhythm, which is normally in and out through the nose. If you're not doing the second type of practice today, but just listen to the recording while engaged in other activities, that's absolutely fine. Just remember to keep a gentle focus on the breathing as you go ahead and listen to the rest of this meditation.

-Just so that you better understand the breathing, we will be focusing on the idea of breathing and the different sensations that can arise from it. Breaths can be calm, relaxed, healthy, and easy for the body when the mind and the surroundings are ideal. Breaths can also be life-altering when the events around you are so important that they change you forever.

-Breathing in through the nose and then out through the mouth a few times now, I want you to focus on the points where the breath is happening. Starting with the top of the nose, the nostrils, the very place where the breath begins, and the air first enters the body. Focus on the very tip of the nostrils now, feel the force of the air as it gets pulled in through the nose.

-As the breath moves further down the respiratory system, feel it go down through the first part of it. Notice the breath physically move down from the nose through the air tubes in the face and then down the chest area, all the way to the lungs. Observe the flow of air as it makes its way through the body without any stress or obstacle.

-And as the breath reaches the lungs, notice how they expand once the air is all inside them. From there, the oxygen will get carried away, thanks to the bloodstream, to every single particle in the body in a series of events that are worthy of a miracle. This is where life starts, just as the oxygen gets transported throughout the body.

-When the air is let out of the body, it gets expelled the same way it came in. The entire body is left without air for a brief moment, just so that it can once again be completely awakened to life by the simple act of inhaling.

-Notice how the air travels from inside your body all the way through the respiratory canals and out through the same tip of the nostrils. Completing the full circle of breathing. Putting life in the body and taking out all that is unnecessary, unpleasant, uneasy, uncanny.

-Let all of the emotions and feelings and thoughts roll out of the system, giving the mind and body space.

-You are doing wonderfully thus far. Before moving on, take a few moments to simply enjoy this new feeling of ease and calm that you've just acquired all throughout the body now.

-And as we move on with the practice today, we'll be focusing on the gentle breath while listening to some powerful affirmations for you. It doesn't matter if you're staying still or moving around, doing whatever you have or want to do today. Listening to these affirmations will completely change the way you'll see the simple breath from now on.

-For most of us, breathing happens mechanically. The body simply knows when to breathe, how to breathe, if it needs to breathe faster or slower. Mindfulness is all about breathing consciously, being aware of the miracle of every single breath. This is why breathing is at the core of most spiritual journeys people have been taking for thousands of years.

-Getting ready to listen to these affirmations, simply regroup your gentle focus on the act of breathing, as you inhale and exhale softly through the mouth.

-Here we go with the first set of affirmations.

-Let's start with the first affirmation. As you listen to these, gently follow your breath and then listen to the words. It will make it easier for you to focus on the messages of these powerful pieces of knowledge.

-One: If you want to conquer the anxiety of life, live in the moment, live in the breath.

If you want to conquer the anxiety of life, live in the moment, live in the breath.

<<PAUSE FOR 5 SECONDS>>

-Nicely done! Anxiety is all around us all of the time. It is a primordial feeling that is supposed to keep us away from harm. Unfortunately, more often than not, anxiety cripples us and makes its way out of the cave in unnecessary times. If you live in the breath, you'll always be able to conquer anxiety and its outcomes before they even manifest.

-For the second affirmation, we'll be focusing on the breath, a gentle, soft, controlled breath. Remember to fully become aware of the words that you're about to hear next.

-Two: Breath is the most exquisite gift of nature. Be grateful for this beautiful gift.

Breath is the most exquisite gift of nature. Be grateful for this beautiful gift.

<<PAUSE FOR 5 SECONDS>>

-Good job. Nature has made us different from the other species in a way that lets us become fully aware of the breaths that we take. We can enjoy the breaths that we take, but we mostly never do so. Why? Because we are so caught up in our minds, we never fully become aware of the breathing. It's a mechanical process, whereas it's supposed to be a gift every time it happens.

-For the third affirmation of the day, we'll be focusing on the message and try to follow it as it is read to us. Become active with the mind and body while listening to what this one has in store.

-Moving along, we've now reached the seventh affirmation of the day, as powerful and as important as the last six. Pay close attention to the next words as you follow your breath.

-Seven: Pause; breathe. Repair the universe, then proceed. Those of us who know how to breathe will thrive.

Pause; breathe. Repair the universe, then proceed. Those of us who know how to breathe will thrive.

<<PAUSE FOR 5 SECONDS>>

-Good. Pausing is important when you do it consciously. When you pause from your game just to look for another one to play later, it's an unconscious, automatic process. It has no real value in your life. When you pause from anything that you're doing to breathe, you repair your status from unconscious and mechanic to conscious and lively. If you know how to breathe properly, consciously, then you will live gracefully and have a great story.

-We're going to be eight affirmations done in just a bit. Listen to this next one gently, while keeping a steady focus on the breath. All right, here we go with this next one right now.

-Eight: Without full awareness of breathing, there can be no development of meditative stability and understanding.

Without full awareness of breathing, there can be no development of meditative stability and understanding.

<<PAUSE FOR 5 SECONDS>>

-Perfect! Meditation, as we've covered it right until now, is based on the simple act of breathing. All you need to do is to become aware of your breath. And only then everything else stops in its tracks. Your movement, actions, thoughts, emotions, feelings, they all stop. Full awareness of breathing is the one true path towards complete meditation, as well as stability and a new level of understanding for your mind and body, of discovery about them both.

-This is going to be our ninth affirmation right now, so we're just two away from the end of the series. I know, it's a little long this process, but trust me, it's rewarding. Let's now listen.

-Nine: Feelings come and go like clouds in a windy sky. Conscious breathing is my anchor.

Feelings come and go like clouds in a windy sky. Conscious breathing is my anchor.

<<PAUSE FOR 5 SECONDS>>

-Good job so far! Feelings can be hard sometimes. You get so caught up in them that you often forget how to live or function well. The thing about feelings is, as is with everything else in life, they're just here for a moment. They pass, just like clouds evaporate in the skies, no matter how many days they block the sun. It will always be there, that blue sky. Why waste your mind by setting it in a wrong way, when you can let it free from worry by choosing to do so?

-We are one affirmation away now. Congratulations for sticking through this entire thing, you're smashing it! Let's listen to this very last one and focus on it, and on the breath.

Ten: Life is a dance. Mindfulness is witnessing that dance.

Life is a dance. Mindfulness is witnessing that dance.

<<PAUSE FOR 5 SECONDS>>

-Nice! Life truly is a dance, but not a typical, rehearsed one. Life is a dance that you've never practiced before, and the music is continuously changing. This is why it's crazy to get so caught up in the circumstances. Instead of always trying to adapt and change because of external factors, it is much better to just witness the dance. Enjoy the dance. Be part of the dance. Embrace the dance of life.

-Perfect, you did great! Once more, please take a few moments to appreciate the state of your entire being right now. Notice how the breath has completely calmed the mind and eased the body. How the simple act of breathing that you've looked upon has changed the way you think and act today.

-And before we move along to the ending part of the meditation, remember that you can always look back to these affirmations and listen to them again, or simply recall them from memory. Whenever things get complicated, and they will, just follow these meditations back to this practice, remember or listen to them again, and take back the control. It's that easy, and it gets easier and more comfortable if you put in the time and the effort to practice it.

-It is now time to end this meditation practice, which we'll be doing by refocusing the mind and body to the external world. Coming back to the present moment simply means noticing the different aspects of the body that will lead you back into the exterior world.

-Begin by noticing the different sounds around you. See what it is that you can hear without trying too much. Is there any sound that's coming from in the house, like maybe a pet playing in the living room, or a pan on the stove in the kitchen? Are there any sounds that are coming from the outside, like cars passing by or even the sound of a jet plane cruising way above your head?

-Continue by engaging your sense of touch. Feel every single pore of skin that is getting touched by the clothes on you. Feel the weight of your body as it presses down into the chair or floor. Whatever it is, just notice the sensation of weight and touch as you slowly pull yourself back from the meditative state.

-Finishing up, gently open the eyes and become fully aware of your surroundings now. See what you can see without making any movement of the head or body. Emerge back into the present state and environment as you dedicate your sight to becoming completely aware of the now.

-We have now reached the end of our practice. Listen to your internal body and be joyful about where you've been today, how calm and relaxed you are, and how valuable the lessons of the day have been for you regarding mindfulness, peace, and breathing.

-And as you go on with your day today, or if it's night, as you go to bed, keep this relaxed, gentle touch of awareness throughout the rest of your activities. Keep a gentle focus on the breathing, of the mind and body, without judging the mind or body, but simply being more aware of both of them all throughout your day.

-Thank you for being a part of this meditation practice. Keep on breathing, and everything, no matter how complicated, will solve itself between the next inhale and exhale. See you again soon. Goodbye!

Before we part, I would like to once again remind you that as a self-publishing author, reviews are the lifeblood of my work. I would be very happy and thankful if you could take a few moments to leave a review on Amazon. I truly appreciate your time.

REFERENCES

Adrian, A. (2016) How to Feel Your Feelings and What That Will Do for Your Life (Everything!). Retrieved from https://tinybuddha.com/blog/how-to-feel-your-feelings/

Aha Parenting.com. (n.d.) About Aha! Parenting. Retrieved from www.ahaparenting.com/about

Amodeo, J. (July 8, 2018) What It Really Means to Be in the Present Moment. Retrieved from https://psychcentral.com/blog/what-it-really-means-to-be-in-the-present-moment/

Anderson, D. (November 28, 2017) For Anxious Salongoers, the Quiet Chair Offers a Less Chatty Option. Retrieved from www.racked.com/2017/11/28/16635662/quiet-chair-hair-salon-mental-health

Babauta, L. (n.d.) How to Meditate Daily. Retrieved from https://zenhabits.net/meditate/

Beach, S.R. (October 21, 2014) Teaching Mindfulness to Teenagers: 5 Ways to Get Started. Retrieved from www.huffpost.com/entry/teaching-mindfulness-to-teenagers_b_5696247

Corliss, J. (January 8, 2014) Mindfulness meditation may ease anxiety, mental stress. Retrieved from www.health.harvard.edu/blog/mindfulness-meditation-may-ease-anxiety-mental-stress-201401086967

Donaldson, F. (January 15, 2017) When Your Mind's Full of Dad Stuff, You Need Mindfulness. Retrieved from http://thedadwebsite.com/2017/01/when-your-minds-full-of-dad-stuff-you-need-mindfulness/

Edberg, H. (March 5, 2019) 8 Ways to Return to the Present Moment. Retrieved from www.positivityblog.com/8-ways-to-return-to-the-present-moment/

Feldman, D.B. (December 19, 2017) Why Daydreaming Is Good for Us. Retrieved from www.psychologytoday.com/us/blog/supersurvivors/201712/why-daydreaming-is-good-us

Fink, K. (November 22, 2016) 10 Mindfulness Techniques For Anxious Moms, That All New Moms Should Know. Retrieved from www.romper.com/p/10-mindfulness-techniques-for-anxious-moms-that-all-new-moms-should-know-22930

Fondin, M. (June 10, 2015) 6 Modern-Day Meditation Leaders You Can Learn From. Retrieved from https://chopra.com/articles/6-modern-day-meditation-leaders-you-can-learn-from

Gaiam: Inner Idea. (n.d.) Meditation 101: Techniques, Benefits, and a Beginner's How-to. Retrieved from www.gaiam.com/blogs/discover/meditation-101-techniques-benefits-and-a-beginner-s-how-to

Headspace. (n.d.) The benefits of daily meditation. Retrieved from www.headspace.com/meditation/daily-meditation

Harrison, P.M. (May 16, 2013) 15 Best Self Help Books And Self Help Gurus Ever. Retrieved from www.thedailymeditation.com/the-top-ten-self-help-and-self-improvement-gurus

James, A. (2018) How to Escape Being a Victim of Time & Truly Live in the Present Moment. Retrieved from www.pocketmindfulness.com/live-in-the-present-moment/

Kane, S. (July 8, 2018) 7 Reasons Why You Need Quiet Time.

Retrieved from https://psychcentral.com/blog/7-reasons-why-you-need-quiet-time/

Katz, B. (n.d.) How to Avoid Passing Anxiety on to Your Kids. Retrieved from https://childmind.org/article/how-to-avoid-passing-anxiety-on-to-your-kids/

Kuegler, T. (May 29, 2018) How To Become Ridiculously Self-Aware In 20 Minutes. Retrieved from https://medium.com/the-mission/how-to-become-more-self-aware-in-under-20-minutes-968268c53ffd

Marcin, A. & Gill, K.R. (August 29, 2019) What is Peaceful Parenting? Retrieved from www.healthline.com/health/parenting/peaceful-parenting

Markham, L. (January 21, 2016) 13 Tips to Transition to Peaceful Parenting. Retrieved from www.psychologytoday.com/us/blog/peaceful-parents-happy-kids/201601/13-tips-transition-peaceful-parenting

Markham, L. (n.d.) 9 simple habits to practice peaceful parenting. Retrieved from www.mother.ly/life/9-simple-ways-to-practice-peaceful-parenting

Mehta, R.; Sharma, K.; & Parashar, B. (May, 2019) Evidence for the Role of Mindfulness in Cancer: Benefits and Techniques. Retrieved from www.ncbi.nlm.nih.gov/pmc/articles/PMC6623989/

Mindful Staff. (October 8, 2014) What is Mindfulness? Retrieved from www.mindful.org/what-is-mindfulness/

Morse, S. (March 4, 2019) Self-Regulation, Connection, and the Principles of Peaceful Parenting. Retrieved from www.azzaschildpsychologyclinic.com.au/blogDetail.php?Self-Regulation-Connection-and-the-Principles-of-Peaceful-Parenting-53

Neal, D.T.; Wood, W.; & Quinn, J.M. (May 26, 2011) Habits—A Repeat Performance. Retrieved from https://web.archive.org/web/20110526144503/http://dornsife.usc

.edu/wendywood/research/documents/Neal.Wood.Quinn.2006.pd
f

Newman, L. (January 11, 2012) Eckhart Tolle: Why You Aren't At
Peace Right Now. Retrieved from
http://www.oprah.com/spirit/why-youre-not-at-peace-yet-how-to-
find-peace-eckhart-tolle/all

Peaceful Parent Institute: Genevieve (2014) Repairing the connection
after conflict with your child. Retrieved from
www.peacefulparent.com/repairing-the-connection-after-conflict-
with-your-child/

Peaceful Parent Institute. (n.d.) The Peaceful Parenting Philosophy.
Retrieved from www.peacefulparent.com/the-peaceful-parenting-
philosophy/

Psychology Today. (n.d.) Laura Markham Ph.D. Retrieved from
www.psychologytoday.com/us/experts/laura-markham-phd

Rahl, H.A.; Lindsey, E.K.; & Creswell, J.D. (March, 2017) Brief
Mindfulness Meditation Training Reduces Mind-Wandering: The
Critical Role of Acceptance. Retrieved from
www.ncbi.nlm.nih.gov/pmc/articles/PMC5329004/

Remski, M. (February 2, 2014) Mindfulness for Fathers: 5 Difficult
Feelings We Can Learn to Love. Retrieved from
www.huffpost.com/entry/mindfulness-for-fathers-f_b_4369337

Self-Control. (n.d.) Retrieved from
www.psychologytoday.com/us/basics/self-control

Selva, J. (February 4, 2020) History of Mindfulness: From East to West
and Religion to Science. Retrieved from
https://positivepsychology.com/history-of-mindfulness/

Silverman, R. & Markham, L. (2017) How to Stop Yelling and Start
Connecting with Your Kids. Retrieved from
https://drrobynsilverman.com/how-to-stop-yelling-and-start-
connecting-with-your-kids-with-dr-laura-markham/

Sovik, R. (n.d.) Lengthen Your Meditation Time. Retrieved from https://yogainternational.com/article/view/lengthen-your-meditation-time

Stibich, M. (February 5, 2020) How to Sit When Learning Meditation. Retrieved from www.verywellmind.com/how-to-sit-when-learning-to-meditate-2224121

Sullivan, K. (n.d.) Attitude of Gratitude: Why Being Grateful Can Improve Every Part of Your Life. Retrieved from www.tckpublishing.com/why-being-grateful-can-improve-your-life/

Tanya. (2018) How do you Rest & Reset your body, mind and soul? Retrieved from www.theroadunseen.com/how-do-you-rest-reset-your-body-mind-and-soul/

Tartakovsky, M. (July 8, 2018) How to Listen to Yourself & Others. Retrieved from https://psychcentral.com/blog/how-to-listen-to-yourself-others/

Taylor, M; Mottweiler, C.M.; Naylor, E.R.; & Levernier, J.G. (June 11, 2015) Imaginary Worlds in Middle Childhood: A Qualitative Study of Two Pairs of Coordinated Paracosms. Retrieved from www.tandfonline.com/doi/full/10.1080/10400419.2015.1030318

The Zen Studies Society. (n.d.) How to Practice Zen. Retrieved from https://zenstudies.org/teachings/how-to-practice/

Thum, M. (August 31, 2008) What is The Present Moment? Retrieved from www.myrkothum.com/what-is-the-present-moment/

Valentine, M. (January 8, 2018) 3 Lessons From the Dalai Lama's Morning Routine. Retrieved from www.goalcast.com/2018/01/08/3-lessons-dalai-lamas-morning-routine/

Villines, Z. (December 22, 2017) What is the best type of meditation? Retrieved from www.medicalnewstoday.com/articles/320392

Vozza, S. (February 26, 2014) Why You Really Need To Quiet Your Mind (And How To Do It). Retrieved from www.fastcompany.com/3026898/why-you-really-need-to-quiet-your-mind-and-how-to-do-it

What is Meditation? (n.d.) Retrieved from https://liveanddare.com/what-is-meditation/

Woodbury, D. (March 17, 2014) Mindfully Remembering That the Present Moment Is All We Have. Retrieved from www.huffpost.com/entry/mindfully-remembering-tha_b_4966971

Printed in Great Britain
by Amazon